Earth Angels

Edition #2

13 Journeys of Triumph

Wisdom with Wings

Writing with JOY Training & Publishing

DISCLAIMER

The intention of Writing with JOY Training & Publishing is to provide inspiration and "food for thought" by sharing personal experiences and life-gained wisdom. Writing with JOY believes that the chapters in this Earth Angels edition are an accurate, honest and personal account of each author's recollections, interpretations and conclusions regarding persons, events and circumstances. However, it is acknowledged that recounted events, circumstances and conclusions are subjective and may or may not be recollected, interpreted or concluded in the same way by all persons.

ISBN – 978-1-7752385-3-9

Writing with JOY Training & Publishing
907 Wild Ridge Way,
Victoria, British Columbia
CANADA V9C 0H1

Earth Angels Series & Movement

The thirteen journeys of triumph in this second edition of the EARTH ANGELS Series are authentic accounts of how each author overcame a loss, addiction, misstep, or hardship... and went on to thrive. These empowering stories will inspire your creativity and resilience when facing your own challenges, and give you insights for counseling a loved one in need.

Read the excerpts from the book (beginning on page vii) to get a sense of the stories. Should you feel a kinship with an author and want to reach out, you'll find bio and contact information at the end of each chapter.

More than simply publishing a book, the authors have started an EARTH ANGELS Movement. Together with readers like you, we are seeding love, hope, inspiration, peace, and kindness around the globe. If you're not already a member, please join the movement at:

www.facebook.com/groups/EarthAngelsMovement

One of our greatest hopes is that when you're finished reading this book, you'll gift it to a friend. One story, one kind act at a time, we will create the world our hearts desire.

13 Journeys of Triumph

13 Journeys of Triumph

Excerpts from
13 Journeys of Triumph

RECLAIMING MY HEART 25

Ana (Dragana) Bjelica

When Ana Bjelica was a little girl, her family immigrated to Canada from a war-torn part of the Balkans, the former Yugoslavia. Annoyed by her parents' stories about the horrors of war, Ana balked at their tales and warnings when she enlisted in the Canadian Military. In her chapter, "Reclaiming My Heart," Ana shares experiences and insights gleaned when she deployed to the Balkans and then Afghanistan as part of NATO peacekeeping initiatives.

Excerpt from Ana's Chapter

"During one mission in Kabul, I was in the back seat of a hot and dusty armored vehicle. Safety regulations mandated that the windows stay closed and that we remain within the vehicle. Wearing a cumbersome, bulletproof vest, I nervously watched the crowded street. Sweating in the heat, I was thirsty and itchy. My loaded rifle was on my knee, the safety catch in place to prevent me from accidentally shooting my foot or a colleague.

As we bumped along on the unkept roads, all I could think about was getting back to the ladies' barracks in time to have my evening shower before the hot water ran out. Like the locals, I started to think in short-term stints.

When our vehicle became trapped in a traffic jam, however, I became highly alert as I watched for weird movements from my side of the vehicle. A colleague did the same on the other side. Within moments, our driver became visibly unnerved and complained of heart palpitations. In Iraq, he'd been part of a convoy where a vehicle had been blown up. He knew that we were a potentially easy target, a sitting duck in a sea of unrest."

THE FREEDOM VOYAGE 41

Arnold Vingsnes

Originally published in *Heartmind Wisdom #2*, "The Freedom Voyage" is a vivid account of when Arnold Vingsnes embarked on a five-thousand-mile voyage from Vancouver, British Columbia to Cedros Island, off Mexico on the Baja Peninsula. When he and the tugboat crew left port, Arnold was looking forward to the adventure of a lifetime. He wasn't disappointed.

Excerpt from Arnold's Chapter

"As we coasted by the South Pacific side of El Salvador, at two in the afternoon, I noticed a target on the radar. We were outside the normal shipping lanes as we sailed close to shore, so had encountered little sea traffic. Grabbing the binoculars, I focused on a small naval ship belching thick black smoke as it came out of the harbor. It was headed in our direction.

Using the intercom, I called the captain's stateroom. 'You'd better get up here. It looks like visitors are headed our way.'

Wearing only underwear and a pair of slippers, the captain entered the wheelhouse and asked, 'What's up?'

I pointed astern. A warship was fast approaching.

'What the hell do they want?' he barked as he grabbed the

second pair of binoculars.

The warship slowed long enough to study the two barges through their binoculars. Then, a great belch of black smoke spewed from their stack. They were making speed our way.

As the distance between us narrowed, their crew donned battle helmets and removed the covers from their cannons. When they swiveled the guns so that they were pointed directly at our little tug, the captain and I screeched in unison, 'What the hell is going on?'"

Brenda Flannery

Brenda Flannery's chapter, "Prescription Nightmare: A Mother's Perspective," is a candid account of her daughter Mindy's withdrawal from Oxycontin and fentanyl, medications prescribed by Mindy's doctors following a car accident.

Excerpt from Brenda's Chapter

"One night, extremely worried about Mindy's emotional state, her stepfather, sister and I took her to the hospital with the hope that they'd admit her to the psych ward and begin weaning her off the medications destroying her life. The Emergency doctor refused to admit her. When we threatened to sue him should Mindy die at home, he finally agreed to keep her for observation.

While she was in the hospital, we learned that the medical system wouldn't cover the $10,000 cost to place Mindy in a detox center. I couldn't believe my ears. The doctors who'd prescribed the potent mixture of narcotics were the ones responsible for my daughter's drug dependency. Whenever a doctor deemed that the effect of the medication had decreased, the dose was increased. Intelligent and wise, Mindy would never have even considered taking street drugs. It was grossly unfair that she had unwittingly become addicted to prescribed narcotics. How was it possible that the curative measure wasn't covered by the medical system?

Unable to afford the cost of placing Mindy in a detox center, she agreed to living with me and her stepfather while she gradually weaned off the drugs. To help us keep track of which medications she needed to take when, the pharmacist at our local drugstore blister-packed the pills. Rather than the usual four rows of daily medication most people take, Mindy's addictive assortment was packaged in eight rows."

Charlene Janzen

Believing that she'd one day marry her Prince Charming, when she was young, Charlene Janzen viewed every occasion as an opportunity to meet him. "Getting ready to leave the house took hours as I ironed my clothes, showered, put on makeup, and styled my hair." In "Cinderella No More," Charlene recounts how her fairy-tale beliefs shaped her expectations, decisions and life.

Excerpt from Charlene's Chapter

"Prince Mark arrived when I was eighteen. He was eight years older than me, wore a black trench coat, and seemed worldly and mysterious. A month after we met, he asked me to marry him. I excitedly accepted his proposal as visions of walking down the aisle wearing a flowing white dress danced in my mind. For the next few months, I lived on cloud nine as I asked my maid of honor and five bridesmaids to stand up with me, selected fancy invitations, ordered a tiered wedding cake, booked the church and minister, chose our wedding rings, and planned the meal that we would serve to the hundreds who'd attend the reception. We married in the summertime one year after we met.

My dream wedding went off without a hitch. I felt lucky, loved and adored by many. We slept in a hotel that night, which was fun until the sun came up and the glow of the wedding began to fade. Both of our families helped pay for our elaborate wedding. Paying for the honeymoon was up to Prince Mark and me. Our savings limited, we decided to go camping at a nearby park in Collingwood, Ontario. The first and only night of our honeymoon, it rained buckets. Our tent flooded to the point that our air mattresses were floating. We gave up and slept in the car. Our marriage went downhill from there."

Gerry Beazely was introduced to Reiki when his dying wife, Sharron, was in the hospital being treated for her long-suffered and severe COPD (chronic obstructive pulmonary disease). Surprised when his wife claimed it was the exact energy healing he'd been giving her for years, he attended a Mother Mary's Healing Circle meeting. It was the first step in meeting that would forever alter the skeptical and conservative man's life.

Excerpt from Gerry's Chapter

"As I began to reach out to friends and family to find my personal Reiki guinea pigs, many surprises came my way. The most dramatic lesson learned was that my extremely religious family, following my mother's lead, firmly believed that energy healing was not an acceptable practice. Somehow, never fully explained to me, it violated one or more of the points of doctrine which they followed. Some of their friends, however, were anxious to take advantage of my services. 'Treating' one of them at a church luncheon almost got me burned at the stake.

My sister's friend, a most willing target of my new talents, was obviously in great pain. Upon hearing of my level one class, he immediately asked for my help. While I worked on him for about twenty minutes, I was totally unaware of the comments of the church community around us. When the fanatical zealots became loud enough to penetrate my focus, I responded in kind. Some of them abruptly left the room after expressing deep concern that my actions were not sanctioned by *powers that be*, whoever *they* may be.

Those in the family who recognized the value of Reiki seemed to expect actual miracles and failed to realize I was a student and they were my 'lab animals,' so to speak. It amazed me that these folks were willing to embrace the idea of energy healing, but only in the context of their strongly implanted religious doctrines."

"This Acorn Didn't Fall Far from the Tree" is a delightful account of the life lessons Jennie Potter learned from her father, some of which were taught via often-repeated mottos. In her chapter, Jennie shares a few of her favorites, including "'Keep it cheap and simple.' (We actually had a T-shirt made up for that one.) In truth, you weren't cheap, you were generous. You took care of those in need, shared windfalls with the family, and opened your doors to acquaintances and strangers needing a meal and a warm bed."

Excerpt from Jennie's Chapter

"You laughed hard at your mistakes. Like the time you put the roof of the shed on upside down. Or when you showered at the villagers' common water station in Nepal. Getting rid of the dirt and the grime from your journey while villagers pointed, laughed and stared, then slowly became hysterical with laughter as a llama peed directly from the ledge above the waterspout onto you. You did not laugh in that moment, you were horrified. But you taught us to look back at life and take humor from mistakes, hardship, and life's twists and turns.

Most times when I think of you, there is a touch of pain with the memory. A loss I still feel. Not just for losing you, but also for my lack of understanding of who you were, until it was too late.

Dad, the loss I felt when you passed was like nothing I'd ever experienced. It was as if I'd been hit by something large, that hit leaving a gaping hole. Near the end, everyone but me knew you were dying. I suppose deep down somewhere, I must have known too. But far deeper than that was the belief that you could never die. You were too strong in life, too big a character. Your stories and laughter boomed in rooms. When you passed away, the hole you left. . .well, let's just say, I realized that you had filled much of the space that shaped and defined me."

LISTEN TO THE WHISPERS 109

Jennifer Marie Luce

"Listen to the Whispers" is an inspiring account of Jennifer Marie Luce's ever-expanding spiritual journey as she recalculated around a variety of happenings including her attempted suicide, ovarian cancer, and romantic relationships. Written in segments, Jennifer Marie shares what she came to know as she journeyed through trauma, hopelessness, disease and change.

Excerpt from Jennifer Marie's Chapter

"The television commercial for the 2017 Jeep Compass was brilliant. In the commercial, you hear the electronic female voice of a virtual assistant say, 'In fifteen meters, turn left.'

A man looks left and continues straight.

The virtual assistant says, 'Recalculating.'

'Go straight to a steady job.'

A woman looks at her workplace, then turns around and heads in another direction.

'Recalculating.'

'Stay single until you're thirty-four.'

A man proposes.

'Recalculating.'

You get the point. The words of the virtual assistant in the commercial represents societal expectations. The actors ignore what's expected and follow their hearts. The premise of the message is that Chrysler (the company that sells the Jeep brand) wants to help you find your true north via the Jeep Compass.

In truth, finding one's true north requires much more than a vehicle or compass."

WELCOME HOME! 129

Josephine Lavallee

Like young people everywhere, Josephine Lavallee endeavored to find her place in the world. As opportunity after opportunity presented, rather than accept her unfolding life, Josephine questioned each happening. In "Welcome Home!," she recounts the consequences and gifts of her rebellious nature as she struggled to fit in at an all-girls school in Interlaken, Switzerland.

Excerpt from Josephine's Chapter

"Late one night, all of us in our pajamas and in our rooms, someone called out, 'I smell smoke.'

'Fire!' bellowed another roomie.

Unnerved, excitement abounded. Six pairs of feet, one behind the other, thumped down the stairs. Switching on the lights, we spotted the wastebasket was on fire, inside and out. The flames, gray smoke and stinky smell startled us. Someone quickly doused the fire with water and took the charred basket outdoors.

Roe, our roomie from Jersey Island, one of the English Channel Islands, had thrown an ignited cigarette butt into the wastebasket before going to bed. It was November, and although smoking wasn't permitted in the chalet, Roe confessed that she'd smoked inside because of the bitterly cold north wind.

After a lively discussion about how lucky we were that Huckleberry had smelled smoke before we all fell asleep, and how we would have been trapped in our rooms with only a small upstairs window as a possible escape route, we all agreed not to tell Principal about the incident. With the sliding glass door open and the upstairs window ajar for ventilation, I went to bed wearing winter socks. Shivering under the duvet cover, deep sleep eluded me.

A few days later, with kindheartedness, we decided Roe should have a new nickname. As she was a good-natured Irish Catholic, we sprinkled her with water droplets as we christened her Sparky. As far I know, she never smoked in the house again.

Fortunately for me, the cigarette episode changed the ambiance in our chalet. Little by little, I discovered that school with dormitory roommates could be hilarious. Letting go of my more serious and uptight self, I was able to be silly once in a while, unlatching a playful side of me I hadn't known existed."

President J. F. Kennedy was assassinated when Joyce Ross was seven years old. Impressed by the extensive news coverage, as others she loved died, Joyce wondered why they didn't receive radio, television and newspaper coverage. Instead, buried toward the back of the local paper, each one's life was marked with an inch-long announcement that included the dates of his or her birth and death, the names of immediate relatives, and the location of the funeral service. In her heart of hearts, Joyce knew that everyone deserved to have his or her contributions recognized, rejoiced and remembered. Newspaper-wise, the space needed to properly honor each one was far more than an inch.

Excerpt from Joyce's Chapter

"Mom and Dad did their best to help us kids understand that dying wasn't necessarily a bad thing, which was why Heaven was only a *possible* final destination. Mom was raised Catholic and occasionally mentioned some places called hell and purgatory, where you didn't want to go but would if you misbehaved too much. Then there was the whole business of Armageddon and judgment day that I learned about at a Saturday afternoon Jehovah's Witnesses Bible school picnic.

I went to the picnic because Mom wanted us to learn about different religions, and because I thought it'd be fun. Which it was, except for the scalding sun beaming down on my hatless head and the foaming dark-brown liquid with bits of white stuff floating around in it that they served in a tall glass at lunch. Certain it had either gone bad or was poison, even when the other kids drank theirs, there was no way I was gonna drink mine. When I later told Mom about it, she said it was an ice-cream float.

As President John F. Kennedy had been shot and killed by a maniac when I was seven years old, I also knew that no matter how famous or important you were, there was no escaping this trip to *Never, Never Want To Go There Land.* At the time, I was in grade two and had made friends with a classmate who'd emigrated from the United States. We were both too young to fully understand the significance of the tragedy, but that didn't stop her from crying when our teacher told us about it.

For the next several days, everyone talked about how sad it was that the U.S. President had been shot. People felt bad for his wife and kids. Even the man who lived inside our radio was upset and talked about it a lot. We didn't have a television, but if the pictures on the front page of the *North Bay Nugget* were an indicator, the people in *TV Land* were probably sad too."

A SPIRITUAL FAREWELL WITH DADDY 167

Karen Reidie-Thorstad

In "A Spiritual Farewell with Daddy," Karen Reidie-Thorstad shared: "Sugar and spice and everything nice, that's what little girls are made of.' I'm not sure I fit into that category; still, I always knew I was 'Daddy's girl.'" Although miles away, Karen was acutely aware of her father's presence as he passed to the eternal side. When his spirit later visited her bedside, tears streamed down her cheeks as she listened to what he'd come to tell her.

Excerpt from Karen's Chapter

"It was June 21st, 1975. My husband, Doug, and I were out on our boat fishing in Finlayson Arm on Vancouver Island. At exactly one o'clock, the song 'My Way' by Frank Sinatra came on radio. An overwhelming feeling of deep loss came over me. As if it were an omen, like the title of the song, Dad always did things *his way*. My eyes welled with tears.

'I think something just happened to Daddy,' I said.

'Do you want go in?' Doug asked.

An unexpected feeling of serenity came over me, and I was aware of Daddy's presence. Having suffered two massive cerebral hemorrhages, my father had been hospitalized for the past nine months. The left side of his body was totally paralyzed, and he couldn't speak. I had witnessed his frustration and anguish many times and could feel that he was now at peace.

Answering my husband's question, I said, 'No, knowing Daddy, I don't think he'd want us to rush in and cut our fishing trip short. I think he would want us to stay out here and enjoy the rest of the day.'

'You know best,' my husband said good-naturedly.

It was a beautiful, sunny day, and I found the ocean calming. After making my way to the bow, I sat at the very tip and watched white waves gently wash against the boat. For the next few hours, I thought about my father and all the things he'd done his way."

TAMING THE INVISIBLE DRAGON 181

Lindsay Laycock-Pirie

It's estimated that one in four people will endure a form of debilitating emotional distress in their lifetime. For Lindsay Laycock-Pirie, that distress manifested in a three-headed invisible dragon that overpowered her thoughts, well-being and life. In "Taming the Invisible Dragon" Lindsay shares how she struggled with and eventually overcame depression, anxiety and agoraphobia.

Excerpt from Lindsay's Chapter

"I was nineteen and living on my own when my dragon morphed into a three-headed nemesis. One afternoon, needing an ingredient from the store for that evening's meal, I opened the door of the apartment and froze as a feeling of impending doom took hold of my being. Every cell in my body filled with fear. My limbs tingled and my legs became weak as my heart pounded within my constricted chest. I could barely breathe. If I left the house something dreadful would happen. Telling myself that I was being silly, I made a few more attempts to leave home, but couldn't.

From that day forward, there were many days I was unable to leave the house on my own. My boyfriend drove me to and from the home where I worked as a nanny. I avoided going out, and spent days trying to psyche myself into attending functions where my absence wasn't an option. While attempting to socialize at one of these events, it was as if I wasn't really present. People would talk and I'd try to listen, but the fear chatter in my head turned their words into gobbledygook. After the function, it would take days for me to feel somewhat calm again.

My family doctor prescribed medication that helped a little. When at home alone, I kept the blinds drawn, the door locked, and often walked laps around the inside the apartment to try and calm myself. Every waking hour of every day, I rode a roller-coaster of fear that peaked and dipped, but never ceased. I couldn't predict what each day would bring. My dragon's third head was officially diagnosed as agoraphobia. At that point, I stopped working."

SECRETS OF BEING ME

Margit Cleven

As a child, not wanting to disappoint them, Margit Cleven kept secrets from her parents. It was a survival technique that followed Margit into her teenage years and adulthood as she sought to emulate her mother's life: happy marriage, healthy kids and a nice home. In the "Secrets of Being Me" Margit shares the upside and consequences of striving to please others.

Excerpt from Margit's Chapter

"When Henry suggested we live together, I hesitated. My parents were churchgoers. It was the late sixties, and older adults viewed unmarried cohabitation as living in sin. Forever a pleaser, not wanting to disappoint my boyfriend, I suggested that the two of us talk to my mother about the idea.

Mom was mortified. After a heated discussion, she made me promise not to tell my dad. When we left my parents' place, Henry drove me back to my aunt's house. Living together wasn't an option. Having witnessed how upset Mom was, I didn't want her to worry or be disappointed in me.

Mom didn’t get the memo. She didn't understand that Henry and I were asking for her blessing, not telling her a foregone conclusion. After we left her house, worried that I might run away, Mom drove around Vancouver searching for me. When she later told me about her search, I asked her why she hadn't simply called my aunt's place. She didn't have an answer.

A few months later, my brother Andy and I rented a basement suite. No longer under an adult's watchful eye, Henry often spent the night. Shortly after we moved in, my dad asked to stay over for a couple of days. He was attending an event in Vancouver, and he didn't want to daily make the commute from home, which was about an hour away.

For the few nights that Dad was there, when it was time for bed, after saying goodnight, Henry exited the suite via the backdoor, walked around the house to my bedroom window, and climbed through.

Months later, when Henry and I officially moved in together, we hid it from my entire family. Mom didn't always telephone before coming to visit. Sometimes she'd just drop by. Thankfully, by then, we lived on the third floor of an apartment with a controlled entrance and no elevator. Mom had to buzz my apartment to get in. By the time she climbed the two flights to our floor, Henry's belongings were hidden.”

VISITS FROM THE OTHER SIDE 207

Tara Diana Nagy

As far back as she can remember, Tara Diana Nagy has *seen, heard, felt* and *known* things without an earthly reason for why she knows what she knows. In "Visits from the Other Side," Tara wrote: "You'd think having this ability would have helped me be the absolute best I could be, but it didn't. When young, being a medium never frightened me, it confused me as I struggled to make heads or tails of what was going on in my mind."

Excerpt from Tara's Chapter

"I've never slept well. Since I was four years old, I've had what others might call 'imaginary friends.' As there was too much going on in my room, when I was little, I would wait until my parents fell asleep and then sneak into their bedroom and curl up on the small blue rug at the side of their bed. When I started school, I went to bed with the light off and the door open. Once everyone else was asleep, I quietly shut my door and played with the visiting spirits until early morning.

Although I didn't recognize the cause of my challenges at the time, not getting enough sleep and having nighttime visitors wreaked havoc on my psyche. I was always anxious and constantly worried. I fretted over my ability to do homework. Sensing that I was different, although I had friends, I worried whether other kids thought I was weird or odd.

I was an adult when I learned it was possible to set boundaries with spirits that choose inappropriate times or places to make their presence known. I also came to know that mediumship is a gift meant to be shared with others through readings, and that though I'm somewhat unique, there are numerous others who possess similar abilities."

Journey #1

RECLAIMING MY HEART

Ana (Dragana) Bjelica

When I was a little girl, my parents and I immigrated to Canada from a war-torn and wretched part of the Balkans, the former Yugoslavia. At that time, Yugoslavia was a stable up-and-coming communist country. It had its economic struggles but was a functioning society by all accounts.

It was the 1960s and Canada and the United States were advertising for laborers. Like thousands of other immigrants wanting to build a better life for themselves, my parents responded. The Canadian Embassy called first. Following a stressful plane ride, we landed in Canada on a fall day with nothing more than a couple of suitcases.

Desperately wanting to be a "real" Canadian, when young, I avoided talking about my birth country. Born in Canada, my siblings didn't share my angst.

My parents were children during World War II and that's all they ever seemed to talk about. War, war and more war. I thought they were annoying with their sad war stories. Then, perversely, when I grew up, I went to war and that's all I thought about.

I joined the military reserves after my beloved husband died. He died young and I was even younger. Bereaved, my whole world turned upside down, I thought a part-time job with the navy reserves would be a fun hobby, something to do to keep my mind off my own tragedy. The training was difficult, and I probably would have quit had war not broken out in my own birth country in the Balkans.

The Canadian military was over there with the rest of NATO. President Clinton was in charge. Having ignored my home culture for most of my life, I was suddenly keenly interested in my personal heritage and obsessed with what was happening. I wondered, "How could an otherwise stable country, one that had even held the Winter Olympics in 1984, be breaking apart through civil war? How was it possible that this multilingual, multireligious industrialized part of southeastern Europe was falling apart in genocide?"

At the same time, the mass killings in Rwanda were happening. It seemed that my own birthland became a ravaged Rwanda with neighbor-against-neighbor, one tribe against the other. Human decency had disappeared, there was nothing but rage. Wanting to help, I begged my navy reserve unit to let me sign up for the NATO peacekeeping initiative.

During training for my first overseas mission to the Balkans, an older female warrant officer warned me, "Nothing can prepare you for the poverty or the desperation you'll see there." As my parents had always talked about war, I thought, "I'll be fine." But as my training progressed, Dad's stories about bombings came to the forefront of my ponderings.

Growing up in stable Canada had turned me into a complacent and naïve princess. When I walked the streets of my beautiful Canadian city, the most I ever worried about was getting hit by a car or slipping on ice. I never worried about getting blown up to pieces or shot.

If I thought I was in pain after losing my wonderful and talented husband, the fracturing Balkan Peninsula (and later, volatile and intense Afghanistan) showed me what serious pain truly looked like. There were moments when I even glimpsed hell, which helped me better understand my parents. I witnessed the unbelievable hatred, violence and devastation as a supposedly mature Canadian. Dear God, my parents had witnessed this insanity as kids!

But hell is not bleak. One of my first glimpses of it was set in some of the finest, most spectacular geography I had ever seen. Southeastern Europe, where some of the worst bloodshed happened, had beautiful waterfalls that shimmered over the greenest of meadows that were filled with the reddest of poppies. Years later, while in an overloaded plane heading to Afghanistan, I watched an awe-inspiring sunrise over the Hindu Kush Mountains. How could such beautiful mountains allow the devil to tread?

Deeply spiritual and religious, I imagined that if I were to call out to God, "Is this acceptable?" the good Lord would answer, "This violence and conflict is how all countries and nations are formed. You'd be mistaken to assume your pretty Canadian city is without sin." Humanity had a shadow side.

I had witnessed one-on-one violence in Canada, but the violence overseas was on a massive scale. It was a cultural and organized destruction. Witnessing such atrocities helped me comprehend the enormity of what had happened during Nazi Germany. From a gang-against-gang viewpoint, we soldiers were part of an organized military gang deployed to a staged "theater." The terrorists/insurgents/combatants (whatever they are called at a specific time) were part of other gangs. War in the Balkans (and later Afghanistan) was beyond tribal. It was empires fighting over territory, reshaping an entire region.

I saw glimpses of what life during war must have been like for my elders when they were children. When the life is bombed out of a country, people revert to a simpler life to secure food, water and shelter. They become hunter-gatherers again. Some hide in caves. Others escape to the forest.

The former Yugoslavia was once filled with sophisticated urbanites that went on skiing holidays in the Alps and tended to nice gardens. It was the same during the 1970s in Kabul, Afghanistan. Once a cosmopolitan city, rather than being shrouded in blue burkas, women wore fashionable dresses and beautiful scarves. There was music and sports. Young men competed in kite flying competitions. (Oh, how I'd enjoyed flying kites as a kid.)

Hell happens quickly, almost overnight. The Afghan people were no stranger to this. The British Empire had been in the region for well over a century, the Soviet Union invaded in 1979, followed by a collection of other Western countries. Each time their homeland came under attack, the people reverted to their ethnic tribal ways. It was the same with my people in the former Yugoslavia.

Wars take away modernity. Any social, economic, scientific or environmental advances are quickly blown away. The beautiful lands lay littered with dangerous rubble, disease and landmines. There are burnt-out buildings and graves in odd places. Pets, children, widows, and crippled men are abandoned to the streets.

In Kabul, by the time I showed up, the beautiful city was in shambles. It was crowded with humankind from numerous countries. There were women in blue burkas, men in white traditional dress, Westerners in ill-fitting suits or macho casual wear. The air was polluted with fumes from poorly maintained automobiles. Beggars and street children were everywhere.

The mentality was "live for today." Except for having many

children as insurance against starvation, no one planned for the future. Male children were more valuable than female; however, every able-bodied person worked, even small children.

Daughters were viewed as being more expensive to raise than sons and were only prized for their ability to bear sons. An infertile wife was quickly replaced. In some places, if you asked a man how many children he had, he would proudly state his number of sons. A man's reputation was ruined if he had no sons. Even if he had a dozen daughters, the man would not mention them. Daughters didn't count.

Sons provided labor or were cannon fodder for war. Black market and war work were the only jobs available to most local boys and men. To help ensure their survival, some parents hedged their bets by placing one son with the Taliban, another with a different violent gang, and a third as a manual laborer with one of the NATO forces.

Ironically, though poorly valued in families, like gold, females were coveted commodities to enemy tribes. Daughters had to be hidden so that they wouldn't be violated or kidnapped. Long ago perfected by Genghis Khan and Alexander the Great, assaulting women not only demoralized one's opponent, it allowed the enemy to implant its own seed.

During one mission in Kabul, I was in the back seat of a hot and dusty armored vehicle. Safety regulations mandated that the windows stay closed and that we remain within the vehicle. Wearing a cumbersome, bulletproof vest, I nervously watched the crowded street. Sweating in the heat, I was thirsty and itchy. My loaded rifle was on my knee, the safety catch in place to prevent me from accidentally shooting my foot or a colleague.

As we bumped along on the unkept roads, all I could think

about was getting back to the ladies' barracks in time to have my evening shower before the hot water ran out. Like the locals, I started to think in short-term stints.

When our vehicle became trapped in a traffic jam, however, I became highly alert as I watched for weird movements from my side of the vehicle. A colleague did the same on the other side. Within moments, our driver became visibly unnerved and complained of heart palpitations. In Iraq, he'd been part of a convoy where a vehicle had been blown up. He knew that we were a potentially easy target, a sitting duck in a sea of unrest.

Unkept children begged and hustled scarves, knives, and other local wares to folks in cars, trucks, motorcycles, bicycles, and camel carts. A boy with dark cropped hair that I'd seen before caught my eye. He was about nine years old, and this time, he was dragging a crying toddler girl (probably his sister) through the clogged traffic. I watched as he pounded on car windows and begged for a few pennies. When no one tossed any coins his way, he cried in frustration, tears streaming down his dusty cheeks. He'd likely be beaten if he failed to meet the daily quota set by his family or his pickpocket bosses.

Later during the same mission, my commander and I were walking along another dusty street. Lightly armed and feeling on edge, I kept a hand on my pistol holster and a watchful eye on the chattering children. They were expert pickpockets. God help me if I returned to base without my pistol. If I did, I couldn't imagine which would be worse, getting captured by the Taliban or being court marshalled for losing my weapon to a bunch of kids.

The children moved like crows among the eclectic crowd of men and a few veiled women. Some of the men were business types, some were rough looking, others were like us, military types from one country or another. Surveying them, I thought,

"That's a United Nations deployment, for you. It's like a scene out of a Star Wars movie. Everyone and their cousin is out there making deals, doing business, patrolling, moving and shaking. If war is hell, then hell is very crowded."

Watching the children peddling their wares reminded me of my dad's stories about being a street urchin in Yugoslavia during the Second World War. I also recalled how annoyed I'd been by his and my mom's warnings that one must be prepared for anything that could go wrong. At that moment, their warnings pounded in my head. War zones were not dead zones. Like a volatile earthquake zone, they were extremely active and could suddenly erupt.

The street urchin kids were smart, cute and incredibly savvy. Interacting with them was frowned upon, and we weren't allowed to purchase the beautiful cashmere scarves that they sold. Each time they pestered us, I shooed them away, trying to sound strict as I clucked at them in my mother tongue (like my mom did when my siblings and I were little). After once such incident, my commander asked, "What did you say to them?" I answered, "I told them to get lost. We don't have any money."

A short while later, when the kids approached us again, my commander bought three scarves, one each for his wife and two daughters. I frowned at him and in a raised voice told the children to scram.

"What?" my commander said, surprised by my aggression.

"Buying merchandise from those kids is poor security. They could steal your wallet, ID, or worse – your pistol!"

He shrugged. Like many of the men I served with, he wasn't concerned about the security risk posed by children. Unlike me, he'd never had to deal with aggressive pickpockets.

Every child on the street belonged to one territorial gang or another. Every child was a potential threat. Pickpockets worked in pairs or small groups. The small ones could be dangerous. Once, while stationed in the Balkans, worried about being knifed, I almost had to pull my pistol on a young boy. He was about twelve and was eyeing me with a menacing, focused glare. Thankfully, my glare and sharp tongue convinced him to scram.

In war zones where I was deployed, civil laws didn't exist or weren't always enforced. Instead, areas were divided into turfs and controlled by gangs. I learned this lesson one sunny day in the Bosnian farmlands when we happened upon a car crash in the middle of nowhere. My colleagues and I considered radioing the local police in a nearby town, but they were rather far away. Minutes later, the local war lord and his people showed up out of nowhere. News travels at lightning-speed in war zones. It might have been the middle of nowhere for us, but it wasn't *nowhere* for the local folk.

Most of the street kids in any war zone were merchants or beggars working on behalf of their families or some crime lord. Civilians, no matter how polite they were to us, were not pleased to have soldiers from foreign countries in their city protecting whatever sitting government the Western forces had put in charge. One day, someone is nice to you; another day, a bomb explodes. Hence, security was always a bit dicey as I tried to decipher who was a potential enemy.

This hard lesson was learned one lovely fall day in Kabul. A couple of female American army officers were scheduled to go to their headquarters (HQ) that day, and they agreed that I could tag along. We thought we would do a girls' lunch out at the HQ chow hall. There was a nice cafeteria there with much better food than the over-fried Tex-Mex fare they fed us at my camp. It would be nice to get away, just us girls.

The American HQ was a couple of kilometers away. I hurriedly prepared various reports for all my commanders, checked the weather, and then the local calendar. It was some kind of public holiday. Suddenly this bothered me. I knew that the local people liked to party on holidays. I also knew what insurgents thought holidays were good for terror.

As we were preparing to leave for our little outing, my gut instinct became too strong to ignore. The weather was perfect. The shops were closed. The locals were off work, and most would be partying in their homes. Armed forces personnel and other non-locals would still be out and about since it wasn't their holiday. Plus, soldiers weren't allowed to celebrate, even if it was. Suddenly it hit me like a lightning bolt. We should not go out to the American HQ that day!

I started cancelling all military personnel outings and advised my girlfriends to reschedule their meeting and not to leave our compound. I then told the locals who were employed as cleaners and interpreters to go home. People were displeased. A few of the soldiers frowned, muttering, "Why is this Canadian going on, telling people what to do?" Some of the men said that I was overreacting. Others told me I was paranoid. I didn't care.

And then it happened. There was a sound of something going off in the distance. It wasn't particularly loud because it was far away, but I knew instinctively what it was. A colleague had told me that when he felt a bomb going off nearby, he thought his teeth were going to fall out. This one wasn't like that, but my skin was tingling, nonetheless.

I listened for a second bang. When I didn't hear one, I made a beeline for our mess hall as my parents' lessons came back to me. Overdone Tex-Mex food notwithstanding, one of the primary fundamentals of surviving a war is ensuring you have food. Our base was about to go into lockdown, and I wanted to make sure that I had enough food for the duration. Sure enough, after I collected a few cartons of fried chicken and doughnuts, the cafeteria was closed as everyone was ordered to their stations.

It wasn't long before reports came in about what had happened. It seemed that a young lad had snuck past the guards close to the American HQ. The kid was about fourteen years old and wired with explosives. His target destination was either the American HQ or the U.S. Embassy a few kilometers further away. Whatever his destination, he had crossed paths with the local gang of street children who were guarding their territory.

We never learned whether the bomb detonated as a result of the suicide bomber's altercation with the street kids or was prematurely set off by the young lad. Whatever the case, it happened, total devastation. Everyone was killed: the street kids, a number of merchants, some beggars and passersby – all of them.

A few days later, when we were allowed out, I wanted to do an assessment of the area. A few colleagues and I visited the blast zone. A good block of the city had been wrecked by the blast. There was broken glass and rubble everywhere. It was not the worst bomb in terms of its power, but it was still very destructive. Had my female officer friends and I left for our luncheon at the planned time, we would have been hit. We would not have survived the blast. We would have gone home in caskets.

A chill went through me as I wondered, "Would I have shot the young lad with the bomb if I'd seen him?" Trained to shoot, it's quite possible, but there was an inherent flaw in such an action. You can't really expect to win when you bring a handgun to a bomb fight.

First, the young suicide bomber would have been difficult to spot. I knew what to look out for, but even if I'd detected and challenged him, it's likely that he would have detonated the bomb anyway. Second, if I'd shot him successfully, the bomb would have exploded. Third, if I by some chance I'd convinced him to abandon his mission, then someone else would have remotely detonated him. (Commonly referred to as a "chicken switch," bombs strapped to a human are often fitted with a switch that can be triggered remotely should the bomber chicken out and flee.) No matter the scenario, my pistol was not a match for any explosive.

Every soldier on the American base was visibly upset by the senseless loss of life. Unfortunately, the rules were such that we were discouraged from getting involved with the locals. A few of my Canadian female colleagues and I decided to breach protocol and help where we could. The least we could do was set up a collection to help pay for the burial of the dead street kids.

One local mother had tragically lost three kids in the bombing. Her children had provided the family income. In her part of the world, there was no insurance, no social services, nothing. Without an income, her family would have no means to buy food. Most childless wives were quickly replaced and abandoned. The idea of this woman starving to death—alone and grieving for her children—was more than we could bear. We had families too.

During the small service for her children, I tentatively approached the grieving mother. When I looked into her shocked and sorrowful eyes, her pain hit me like a brick. Women in the area aged quickly and I could tell that she was nearing the end of her childbearing years. She would soon be too old to replace the children she had lost, which would make her a less valued commodity in her husband's eyes.

The Canadian female soldier who had organized this small service told us that if we had cash donations, she would coordinate with a local, trusted grocer to provide for pre-paid food for the grieving mother. Apparently, this woman's husband was a nasty character who had already stated that he intended to find a younger wife. He had also demanded that any cash his wife received be turned over to him as it was rightfully his. When I heard this, my anger boiled. *To hell with men and their stupid laws and their stupid wars.* When no one was looking, I slipped this poor mother a few dollars.

"Was she grateful?" one of my male colleagues later asked. My response was, "Grateful! There was no gratitude on her face, only shock and devastation." His question reminded me of a military tactic referred to as "shock and awe" where displays of spectacular force are used to paralyze the enemy. From my perspective, there wasn't any awe in war, only shock and debilitating grief.

My colleagues and I were far more privileged than the people we watched over. Provided we weren't shot dead or blown to pieces, all of us could count on going home safe and cared for, even if we were injured or sick. Soldiers had insurance and were provided for medically and financially by our home militaries. But there was nothing we could do about any of the locals that worked for us. The reality was that in war-torn countries, disabled men, women and children were often abandoned and left to survive on their own. Orphaned children were often sold off to a gang for "employment." The young suicide bomber might have once been such a kid.

Months later, when I returned home, I hung about my unit feeling listless and bored. My energy was zapped. The suffering I'd witnessed haunted me. I wondered whether the mother who'd lost her children was still alive. Had the desperate young lad I had seen dragging his sister through the traffic managed to beg enough money to avoid a beating that day? Would he live long enough grow up? Would his little sister?

Safe in my nice city, things that had once bothered me seemed trivial. I was no longer interested when my colleagues bantered about internal office politics and promotions. I had pressing personal issues to ponder. My parents, elderly and sick, were no longer living together and wanted me home. My mother wanted to move in with me. My blind father was quite ill, and I needed to buy another home to accommodate him. When some of my disgruntled male colleagues started to talk about retiring, I suddenly took interest.

I was married to my career, but nothing seemed to matter much any- more, not even promotions or pay raises. I had actually thought that I would be promoted and then soon realized that my overseas missions and hard work did not count for much. I grumbled about it for a bit, but my passion for serving was gone. When word came that three of my American colleagues who were still overseas had been killed by a roadside bomb, something inside me snapped. Heartbroken over yet more senseless deaths, I prepared my retirement papers.

After leaving the service, my body hurt everywhere. My health was poor. My mind seemed to be turning to mush. My pocketbook took a substantial hit. Thankfully, I was insured and had savings and investments. Unlike my female counterparts in the Balkans and Afghanistan, I was able to ditch war and return to my well-organized civilian life. Even though I was widowed and childless, in Canada, I still had value as a person and was a capable breadwinner.

Haunted by the woman who'd lost three kids, I thought about the death of my husband. While sick, he'd been well cared for by a loving family and medical staff in a modern hospital. We had public health insurance. The local people that I met overseas had nothing by comparison. That poor woman's children were rubble on the street. Roadkill. How does one recover from that? That was real pain, real grief. Yes, I'd lost my husband, but it was time to let go of the bitterness I'd held onto since he became ill and died.

"What are you going to do?" asked one of my close friends.

Thinking of a person I knew who sold insurance, I answered, "Maybe I'll become an insurance broker." Insurance was about risk assessment and I was good at that.

"But there's no money in it," warned my friend.

What she said was true, war was more profitable. But I did not want to study war anymore.

In many parts of the world, insurance means having many children so that a few (preferably boys) can survive to adulthood and take care of the parents when they are old. Throughout the ages, we humans have always sought insurance against the many risks that threatened our short lives. We also seem to be biologically programmed to protect current and future generations. In modern Western economies, we accomplish this by seeking high-paying jobs and saving or investing money. However, most people on the planet do not have a stable income. In fact, many do not even have basic human rights. Women and children are especially vulnerable, but so are older and disabled men.

Most Canadians feel fairly secure in their clean and civilized suburban neighborhoods. But like many of the local people I met during my army boot travels, anyone's circumstances can change. Without warning, a person can become disabled, or lose a parent or a child. If a deceased person was the primary bread-winner and didn't have life insurance, his or her family will hit poverty like a crash on a highway.

Nowadays, I hang out at my insurance office. I tell people that I'm in risk management. I make less money than I did in the war industry, but I don't think about war much anymore. Instead, I talk about what can happen when a parent dies or when a child becomes sick or when there is an accident. I advise my customers to take such risks seriously and get insurance.

Some of my young clients think I fret too much. Whenever someone complains about the cost of insurance premiums, I say, "Canada has some of the best insurance plans in the world. You could be living in a country that doesn't have that." Newer Canadian immigrant clients usually nod in agreement. They know what I'm talking about.

If I could go back to those war zones as a superhero, I would. Maybe in a parallel universe, I'm doing just that. But in this world, I calculate the cost of disability and death and provide insurance options. I can't prevent wars or eradicate poverty, but I can encourage my fellow citizens to take risks seriously. Every time I help someone plan for their retirement or save for their children's education a small piece of my heart starts to heal. And maybe that's my way of saving the world. Who knows?

About Ana (Dragana) Bjelica

Ana Bjelica lives in Victoria, British Columbia. She studied English literature and writing at the University of Victoria. She served in the naval branch of the Canadian Armed Forces for fifteen years. After retiring, Ana joined the insurance and financial industry. She is currently a wealth protection advisor at a local credit union and provides personal insurance and group benefits for individuals and businesses.

Ana enjoys music, books, literature and fine art.

Connect with Ana (Dragana) Bjelica
E-Mail: anabee100@yahoo.com

Journey #2

THE FREEDOM VOYAGE

Arnold Vingsnes

I'm going!" I shouted.

It was late spring 1976. I was twenty-five years old and working as a deckhand for a tugboat company in Vancouver, British Columbia. A small crew of eight other men and I regularly towed barges from Western Canada to Cedros Island, off Mexico on the Baja Peninsula. When the boss asked for paid volunteers to deliver two newly built oil barges to Puerto Barrios, Guatemala my heart rate increased a few knots. I loved the sense of freedom sailing gave me. This was my chance to voyage along the Central America coastline, through the Panama Canal, and on to the Caribbean. It would take a month to travel the five thousand miles there and the same to get back. I was certainly up for this adventure of a lifetime. Especially since it meant that I'd bank enough leave-time to take most of the winter off with pay.

We left port on a glorious night, the barges lined up perfectly behind us. The ocean was calm, and the heavens were alight with millions of flickering stars. With not a ripple to be seen anywhere, the gentle roll from port to starboard made it a perfect night at sea. The vibration and constant rumbling of the engines blended melodiously with the swishing sounds of the parting waters. Occasionally a dying star would streak across the heavens and then disappear into the darkness. The harmonious teaming of man with nature was one reason I'd become a seaman.

Rounding Cape Flattery at the tip of Washington State, we headed southward. "Gone South" seemed an appropriate name for our coastal tug. However, our boat wasn't outfitted or designed for the tropics. How would she and our reduced crew of seven hold up in the extreme weather and scorching heat?

Four months earlier, a 7.5 magnitude earthquake in Guatemala claimed 23,000 lives, injured over 76,000 and destroyed much of the country, shoreline and ports. The disaster triggered an unprecedented amount of self-organizing in outlying areas, some of which was viewed as anti-government and apparently linked to guerilla organizations. Would the country's escalating civil unrest put us in peril when we reached our final destination?

As dawn broke, the sky erupted in a brilliant crimson mantle. In the North Pacific, the adage "red sky in morning, sailors take warning; red sky at night, sailors delight" was often an accurate weather indicator. Sure enough, the barometer fell steadily as the north-westerly wind climbed to a brisk thirty knots with gusts up to forty.

By noon, the gray hazed ocean heaved with rolling whitecaps. Though it wasn't exactly fair weather with following seas, the wind was behind us, the waves rolling southward with us. We heaved up and down as the swells rolled under the tug. By late evening, on a shift break and down below, I felt the occasional jerk on the tug's towline as the barges lumbered behind us. By midnight, the wind had increased to a steady forty-five knots with gusts to fifty.

Going on watch, I headed for the wheelhouse to check with the captain. Ever so slightly pulling back on the throttle, he ordered, "Better run a bit of line. We need more distance between the tug and the barges."

Mid-vessel by the winch controls, I glanced over the side. The sea frothed with breaking whitecaps that curled up and rushed forward along the hull. The ocean flowed across the aft deck near the stern, occasionally burying the bulwark railing along each side. Shivering, I adjusted the tow line and then checked the rigging. The wind produced an eerie moaning sound as it whipped around the steel cables, but nothing was loose.

Six days later when we reached the San Diego coastline, the weather turned calm, sunny and hot. There was a navel exercise area clearly marked on our navigation chart, so we weren't surprised to see the US Navy in full battle dress as we entered their waters. As there was no notice to mariners that the area was off limits to civilian traffic, we continued on. Suddenly, our tug's navigation and communication equipment malfunctioned. Fiddling with the knobs and switches, I muttered, "What the hell?"

The captain and I checked the radar, startled to note a barrage of airborne speeding objects headed our way before the screen went blank. We hurried out of the wheelhouse and glanced up and around. There were low flying fighter jets in the sky, choppers directly overhead and battleships surrounding us. But the tug wasn't damaged.

Back in the wheelhouse, the radar screen lit up again. More mock missiles sped our way before the screen went blank. We assumed we'd unwittingly become part of their naval exercise, but the atmosphere on the tug was still tense. Receiving no orders to stop, we sailed on as their simulated missiles continued to dart across our radar screen. Several nail-biting minutes later, we exited their exercise area. It was still three thousand miles to the Panama Canal.

One afternoon while asleep in my bunk, I was tossed sideways, my face plastered against the bulkhead. The tug was heeled over on its side and the engines had been throttled down. As I leapt out of my bunk, the tug righted. and the engines geared up. I scrambled up the narrow stairs to the deck to find out what was going on. Most of the crew members were in the wheelhouse staring sternward. I looked at the captain and asked, "What happened?"

"We ran into a whale. I didn't see it until we were on it." Shrugging, he checked with the chief engineer to make sure everything was okay with the engines. Apparently, all was fine.

We were just off Cedros Island, a few miles offshore from the Baja Peninsula, Mexico. The sun was high in the sky and there wasn't a ripple on the ocean. It was obvious to everyone that the captain must have fallen asleep at the helm. As the captain was a self-righteous and belligerent man, no one, including me, was going to suggest such a blunder.

Hoping the whale was okay, I headed back to my bunk. The sunbaked steel hull would mean that my room was now far too hot for sleep, but at least I could rest until my shift.

Needing to refuel the tug, we drifted a mile-and-a-half off of Cabo San Lucas. Shortening the towline so that both barges were together, the captain brought the tug alongside the lead barge where the marine diesel was stored. Noting blue sharks and hammerhead sharks in the water below, my fellow deckhand and I were careful not to fall overboard as we leapt onto the barge. Opening the door to the engine room, my heart sank. The engines were completely under water. There was no way we'd be able to use them to pump fuel into the tug.

Using the tugboat's engine and pumps, our engineers managed to refuel. With both barges' engine rooms still full of ocean water, we headed south.

As we got underway, the captain remarked, "Stupid buggers at the shipyard must have screwed up the venting system so that the following sea we had before San Francisco let the water vent back into the engine room. There can't be any other explanation for it."

"I think you're right, Cap," I said. "I doubt the new owners will be very impressed."

Three hours later, I was steering the tugboat when I heard a commotion on deck and someone hollering, "Stop! Stop! There are turtles in the water."

Peering over the side, I spotted two large turtles bobbing on the surface, one on top of the other as they mated. Knocking back the engines, I made a wide circular sweep, keeping my eyes focused on the turtles and the barges as they arched behind us.

The captain stormed up the stairwell and into the wheelhouse. "What the heck is going on?"

Pointing to the turtles, I quickly explained what had just happened.

"We're heading north, Arnold. Not south! We'll never get to Panama like this."

He was obviously angered by what he likely viewed as crew silliness. But when he spotted the cook and engineer on the outside of the bulwark railing readying to catch the turtles, he seemingly had a change of heart. "Okay, okay. Let's check this out."

The two of us joined the crew to watch as the cook and an engineer managed to grab the turtles and heave them onto the deck. The glorious creatures must have weighed forty pounds each.

"Turtle soup!" shouted the cook as he dashed off toward the galley.

No one moved.

Seconds later, the elated cook returned with a butcher knife clutched in his fist.

He was about to stab the poor turtles to death!

I grabbed the startled turtles and flung them overboard. They quickly dove out of sight.

"What did you do that for?" the cook asked, appearing perplexed and disappointed. "I was going to make us a nice surprise."

Not wanting to get into it with him, I headed back to wheelhouse. I liked the cook. Even though he was drunk by suppertime every day, the man conjured up decent meals and always had a smile. The captain must have liked him too because our ship was supposed to be dry. If any of the rest of us had been caught drinking, we'd have ended up as shark food.

With light winds and sunshine, the sea stretched out before us like a giant unbroken mirror. But as we continued down the Mexican coast, it grew unbearably hot. Without air conditioning and only one ventilation fan between the crew accommodations and galley, living and working inside was intolerable. At night, some of the crew slept on deck in makeshift hammocks. As the heat of the day skyrocketed, crew members' tempers grew shorter and shorter, except for the cook's. He was always cheery.

With daytime temperatures hovering just over a hundred Fahrenheit, the tug's engine room became too hot for us to run at full speed without overheating. Whenever an engineer would go below to check the gauges and fluid levels, they'd be back within five minutes, drenched with sweat. If the engines broke down, it would be impossible for the engineers to withstand the heat long enough to fix the problem.

As we coasted by the South Pacific side of El Salvador, at two in the afternoon, I noticed a target on the radar. We were outside the normal shipping lanes as we sailed close to shore, so had encountered little sea traffic. Grabbing the binoculars, I focused on a small naval ship belching thick black smoke as it came out of the harbor. It was headed in our direction.

Using the intercom, I called the captain's stateroom. "You'd better get up here. It looks like visitors are headed our way."

Wearing only underwear and a pair of slippers, the captain entered the wheelhouse and asked, "What's up?"

I pointed astern. A warship was fast approaching.

"What the hell do they want?" he barked as he grabbed the second pair of binoculars.

The warship slowed long enough to study the two barges through their binoculars. Then, a great belch of black smoke spewed from their stack. They were making speed our way.

As the distance between us narrowed, their crew donned battle helmets and removed the covers from their cannons. When they swiveled the guns so that they were pointed directly at our little tug, the captain and I screeched in unison, "What the hell is going on?"

Glancing aft, I noticed we were not flying the Canadian flag. We'd taken it down during the first storm so it wouldn't be torn to shreds. The Port of Registry was clearly marked on the barges as Guatemala. The men on the warship had no idea who we were or what we were up to.

I sped to our signal flag cupboard, grabbed the Canadian flag and made a mad dash for the stern. It took what seemed like an eternity to fasten the flag to the lanyard and hoist it. By then, there was a mere thousand feet between us, making the warship seem humongous.

Back in the wheelhouse, I looked through the binoculars. Raising our flag had caused a flurry of activity on their deck. A man who was likely their captain gave an order, and a sailor scurried down a ladder and disappeared. A few seconds later, a large book in hand, the sailor returned and scurried up the ladder.

As we nervously waited, their captain flipped through the book's pages, several times stopping to glance our way. Eventually, he saluted us, gave more orders and the guns swung back into locked position. The incident was over.

One morning as we sailed by Honduras, we awoke to find the deck littered with five-inch-long flying fish. Examining them, we noted that they had elongated fins. Perhaps their fins allowed them to propel themselves out of the water and onto the tug.

Later that day, we encountered schools of yellow and black sea snakes. Aware that numerous venomous species inhabit tropical waters, we didn't examine the snakes.

As we approached the border between Nicaragua and Costa Rica late one evening, a magnificent, beautiful and uncanny lightning show lit up the night. For over two hours, from horizon to horizon, vertical and horizontal brilliant bolts of light flashed across the sky. None of us had ever seen anything like it. Although unnerving, it was a breathtaking display of nature's power.

Light on fuel near the south end of Costa Rica, the captain decided to tuck into the Gulf of Dulce. His plan was that we'd scout out a cove, away from the ocean swell, so we could safely bunker up from the fuel barge. Without official clearance to stop and refuel, the crew prepared for a quick turnaround should we be detected and unwelcome.

We were strapped alongside the lead barge, hoses connected and about to begin pumping fuel, when a small speed boat appeared in the distance. Peering through the binoculars, the captain advised us that the boat headed our way was painted grey and the three male occupants were wearing uniforms. With no other choice, we waited for them to reach us.

As the boat drew alongside, the uniformed men waved their hands and yelled at us in Spanish. It was obvious that they wanted to know who we were and what we were doing. None of our crew spoke Spanish.

Within seconds, they lashed their boat to the tug and climbed aboard. They weren't armed, but were obviously military or police. Though they couldn't shoot us, they could definitely make our lives difficult.

Using hand signals and yelling, they made it clear that we were to stay put and not move. They then rummaged through the tug, confiscating all of our magazines and signal flags. After gesturing that they were leaving, but would be back, they climbed into their boat and sped off. It was obvious that they expected us to wait until they returned.

The second their boat slipped out of sight, we disassembled the hoses, ran the tow line out, and got the hell out of there.

We reached the Port of Balboa in Panama on our thirty-second day at sea. As prior arrangements had been made for dock space, we didn't have to anchor offshore. Judging by the numerous other ships awaiting passage through the canal into the Atlantic, we would have to wait our turn.

The captain contacted our shipping agent and the Balboa Port authority for clearance and docking instructions. Once docked, three Custom and Immigration Officers came aboard. A short while later, the paperwork was completed. We would be ferried through the canal together with a smaller eastbound ship. Our wait would be two days.

The captain called our shipping agent in Panama for U.S.

dollars for the crew, and perishables and dry goods to replenish our onboard supplies. Having been cooped up on a tug for over a month, the crew was anticipating a little shore leave while we waited our turn in the canal. Taking shifts so that there was always someone onboard to man the radio and maintain a security watch, each of us would be able to get the better part of a day off.

When he brought our supplies and cash, the shipping agent told us that tensions were high ashore. *Panamanians* were unhappy that the United States controlled the Panama Canal Zone. The previous week, an officer aboard a Norwegian cruise ship had been severely beaten, stripped of his uniform and left for dead on the side of the road. Occasionally, the rebels lobbed grenades and other explosive at passing ships.

The shipping agent warned us that while on shore we should stay inside the five-mile-radius of the Canal Zone where the U.S. military was patrolling on foot and by helicopter. He also gave us a map of the area and a list of restaurants, bars and tourist sites.

Curious and not easily intimidated by potential dangers, once on shore, I headed outside the Canal Zone. How dangerous could it be?

In contrast to the pristine buildings and surroundings within the Canal Zone, the area just outside was rundown and unkempt. Laundry hung from the balconies of the old, narrow, wooden row houses. Apartment buildings that were once painted brilliant white were stained brown and grey. The streets were narrow and dirty. Broken storefront windows were left that way or boarded up. The cars, trucks and motorcycles parked along the streets were older models. The people were obviously poor.

Wandering down an alley in the hot and humid town, though I didn't encounter anyone with guns or grenades, I could sense danger. Awestruck by the vast difference between this country and Canada, I felt fortunate to live in a homeland that was orderly and safe. A few seconds later, I was grabbed from the back, one powerful hand under each of my arms. A deep voice said, "Get in the jeep!"

I jerked my head from left to right. They were U.S. military police. "Do you know where you are?"

Stunned and frightened, I didn't move a muscle.

"If you had reached the end of this alley, you wouldn't have come back."

When one of them gave me a slight push toward the jeep, I got in. It was a quiet and humble ride back to the Canal Zone.

Once back on ship, discussing the last leg of our journey with the captain, I inquired, "Did you order whisky and cigarettes? We'll likely need them to pay off the authorities and their entourage in Guatemala."

"Absolutely not," he bellowed.

It wasn't the answer I was expecting.

"Did you order fans for the crew?" I asked. "We're going to be bucking strong easterlies in the Caribbean. There won't be many opportunities for the men to get relief from the heat on the outside deck. They'll be stuck in the scorching hot hull."

"Screw the fans," he said and walked away.

I called our shipping agent and ordered seven fans, three cases of Johnny Black Label Scotch and two cases of cigarettes. Having just completed three years of voyages to Cedros Island, Mexico, I was well aware that payoffs were traditional and expected. From Customs and Immigration Officers and the Chief of Police to their cousins, distant relatives and hangers-on, everyone expected to be bribed with whiskey and cigarette. It was their customary way of doing business. Otherwise, delays and problems were guaranteed.

When the goods arrived, red-faced and with his chest puffed out, the captain bellowed, "Who the hell ordered this?" Without waiting for an answer, before storming off, he finished with, "This is going in *my* stateroom and no one better touch it."

Thinking of our cheerful cook, I agreed that the captain's stateroom was the safest place to store the booze and smokes. Though, as the crew had searched for and never found the cook's booze stash, if he were to steal the whiskey and hide it, we'd likely never see it again.

The next day, with only one barge behind our tug, the canal pilot onboard took charge and pushed the throttles to full speed ahead as we started toward the first set of locks.

"You can't do that!" our captain shouted. "You're going to break the lines."

"In the Canal Zone, I'm in charge," the pilot bellowed. "If I want full speed, then full speed it is. We have schedules to meet. If the lines break or anything else goes wrong, if need be, I'll drive this tug and barge up on the beach. Nothing *can* or *will* impede traffic in the Canal."

With the lines stretched singing tight, we headed for the Miraflores locks. In two stages, the locks would elevate us eighty-five feet and into Gatun Lake. At the eastern end of the lake, a triple flight of locks would lower us into the Atlantic.

Tucked in behind a small Russian freighter, tethered to small onshore locomotives on each side, we were dragged through the locks. Our ascent from the Pacific side and our descent into the Atlantic went like clockwork. Our next trip through with the second barge was equally impressive and exciting.

We refueled at Colon, Panama, this time, *with* permission.

Sailing the Caribbean, we set course for Jamaica, the Cayman Islands and finally Puerto Barrios. This semi-circular route would avoid the reefs and shoals along the coasts of Nicaragua and Honduras.

A steady twenty-five knot easterly slowed us down and made the passage uncomfortable but manageable. It was hotter than hell. Blankets of sea spray and steady bucking made it impossible to sleep on deck. As it was much like being in a bouncing sardine can with someone holding a blowtorch to its sides, it was equally impossible to sleep in the crew accommodations.

It took seven days to reach Puerto Barrios, Guatemala. Without a pilot, we made our way to the only pier in sight. Through the binoculars we could see that the concrete dock's surface was upheaved in spots. The damage was likely caused by the recent earthquake.

Further along, we spotted a small coastal freighter unloading cargo, one sling at a time. It looked like we could slide in right behind it. With our barges lashed together and on a short line, we maneuvered our way to the inside of the dock. As we rounded the corner, we could see that the freighter occupied the only safe place to tie up. The rest of the dock on that side was in rough shape. Tying up on the other side of the pier was our only option.

The minute we were tied-up, we spotted a troop of officials marching our way. A Customs Officer, Immigration Officer, Mayor, Chief of Police, our shipping agent, and the owner of the barges we'd just towed climbed aboard the tugboat. A couple of characters who were seedy enough to be bandits remained on the dock.

Knowing what was expected, we set the stage for the unofficial Customs and Immigration dance: whiskey on the galley table, ice from the freezer, and glasses all around. It wasn't long before the mood went from somber to jovial.

Taking the captain and me aside, the shipping agent informed us that the port wasn't safe. Apparently, local revolutionaries routinely clashed with the military. If we wanted to go ashore, the Immigration Officer would provide us with passes. But if anyone lost his pass, he would be denied re-entry into the dock area. The shipping agent also recommended that we hire a couple of local guards to stay onboard and keep an eye out for potential problems.

When we agreed to hiring guards, the two seedy looking characters were ushered onboard. One guy came up. The other ran the opposite way on the dock. He returned ten minutes later with ammunition clips and an automatic rifle slung over his shoulder. Positioning himself at the bow, he prepared to keep watch over the tug.

When we asked the shipping agent what we should pay the guards, he said they'd be happy with the half-dozen empty forty-five-gallon fuel drums on the barges, a few packs of cigarettes, a bottle of whiskey and food while they were onboard. We readily agreed.

Once the official paperwork was completed the captain assembled the crew in the galley for a meeting. "Okay, everybody," he said. "We need to maintain a security watch, so half the crew needs to remain onboard at all times. When it's your turn to go on shore, be careful. It could be dangerous. We'll split leave into two twenty-four-hour periods. But first we need to get the towing gear off the barges and stowed away. It's coolest in the morning, so starting at six a.m. I want all hands on deck. Until then, regular watches will be maintained."

With the shipping agent translating, the captain told the owner that the engine rooms on both barges were full of seawater. When he learned that engines and electronic panel were flooded, the barge owner flipped out. Eventually convinced that the problem would be covered by his insurance company, he calmed down. The captain's gift of cigarettes and whiskey helped to smooth the last of the owner's ruffled feathers.

That evening, I ventured up the dock past the freighter that was still unloading cargo, one sling at a time. A twenty-foot high fence topped with razor wire separated the dock area from the rest of the shore. Scowling armed military guards were stationed at the gate. Outside the dock area, I could see additional military personnel and a few shady looking characters milling around. Though I was looking forward to a little R and R, the scene made me wonder whether I'd enjoy my day off.

On the way back to the tug, a young fellow came down the freighter's gangway and motioned me over. "Wanna buy some great dope?" he muttered in broken English.

"Sorry, not interested." I resumed walking.

The next morning while sitting in the wheelhouse, I watched as a group of military police boarded the freighter. A few minutes later, they came down the gangway with the young fellow who'd tried to sell me dope. Their prisoner was shackled. When they reached the dock, the police took turns striking him. There was nothing I could do.

On shore leave, I quickly noticed that the area of Guatemala around the docks was dingy, run down, littered with military men, and downright scary. After one beer in a local tavern where it seemed every pair of eyes was shooting daggers my way, I went back to the tug.

The next day, we set sail for home. With the exception of a few encounters with nasty weather, it was a much welcomed uneventful voyage. I'd had enough adventure for a while. The ocean wasn't always bluer on the other side.

When we left port in B.C., what intrigued me most about exploring new lands was the sense of freedom that came with it. Returning home, I was filled with gratitude for my precious homeland, family and friends. It was heavenly to think of drifting to sleep in my own bed in a temperature controlled room, belly full and without fear of being tossed awake and my face plastered against the wall. I looked forward to meandering along our litter-free streets, day or night, without fear of repercussion from revolutionaries, police or military. In Canada, I wasn't helpless when it came to police brutality. Should I witness some poor lad being shackled and beat, I could report the event without fear of repercussion for myself. At home, I had the very freedom I'd once thought only sea travel could bring.

About Arnold Vingsnes

Arnold Vingsnes is a co-author in several anthologies. From technical industry-specific submissions for government agencies (including the Human Rights Commission) to poetry, novellas and novels, Arnold has been actively writing all of his life. Unfortunately, many of his manuscripts have been misplaced or lost over time.

Nonetheless, Arnold's varied career—from that of a commercial fisherman, marine officer and captain, trade union leader, business owner, teacher, and management consultant—has provided a vast resource of life reminiscences from where many of his writings emanate. The many accounts of his seagoing and trade union adventures are currently being incorporated into an autobiography.

Arnold lives in Coquitlam, British Columbia where he continues to provide labor relations and human resources consulting services. Arnold is available for select consulting and speaking engagements.

Contact Arnold by e-mail: arnoldvingsnes@hotmail.com

Journey #3

PRESCRIPTION NIGHTMARE: A MOTHER'S PERSPECTIVE

Brenda Flannery

Call it intuition, call it a gut feeling, call it a message from an angel, a sense of dread weighed heavily on my mind. I knew that my beautiful, vibrant, fifteen-year-old daughter, Mindy, shouldn't go to the movies with her friends that evening. It had started to snow. The roads would be slippery. Every bone in my body warned me that if she went out, something horrible would happen.

Unable to offer any tangible proof of my premonition, when my daughter and I got into a heated argument, I relented and let her go out with her friends. A while after she left, I was on the phone with my cousin when I heard the call-waiting beep. Putting my cousin on hold, I took the call. It was a paramedic. My daughter had been in a bad car accident. Unable to tell me the extent of her injuries, the paramedic advised me to meet them at St. Joseph's Hospital.

Every mother's nightmare had come true for me. Scared and needing support, I called Gary Williams and asked him to meet me at the hospital. A longtime family friend, my daughter called him Uncle Gary. If I fell apart, he'd know what to do. Located near our residences in Courtenay, British Columbia, we both arrived at St. Joseph's before the ambulance. When the paramedics wheeled my daughter into Emergency, my heart thumped harder as my world went into slow motion.

Mindy was covered in blood. Completely still, silent and her eyes closed, I couldn't tell if she was conscious or unconscious. Her head and neck braced between padded blocks, on a spinal board, and strapped to the gurney, her injuries were likely serious. Hospital staff rushed to her side, and she was whisked into an exam room. As she disappeared from sight, I wished she'd been able to say, "Hi, Mom." Those two little words would have told me that my daughter would be okay. That I'd be okay.

As the minutes slowly ticked into hours, Gary helped limit the number of times I pleaded with the nurses to let me see my daughter. After what seemed an eternity, I was allowed into her room. She was awake and groggy. The prognosis was that she had a fractured vertebra in her lower back. The doctor called it a seat belt injury and said my daughter would need to remain immobile in bed for eight weeks while it healed. The blood was from trauma to her nose.

Stepping into advocacy mode, I insisted that my daughter be examined by a spinal cord specialist. As there wasn't one in our small town on Vancouver Island, she was medivacked by air to Vancouver General Hospital. Thank goodness I stood my ground. The VGH doctors determined that in addition to breaking her lower back, she had a ruptured bowel, a broken nose and a fractured orbital socket.

A surgeon explained that my daughter's back wouldn't heal on its own. They needed to operate, and using screws, attach a rod to her vertebrae. Her ruptured bowel also needed to be repaired before its leaking contents caused sepsis, an infection that could kill her. That surgery would determine whether she'd need a colostomy bag to collect her body's waste.

I burst into tears. Having a "poop bag" strapped to her side would devastate my beautiful daughter. A day earlier, she'd been happy, energetic and full of life. Now, she was lifelessly still, her future uncertain. Various medications dripped into a main artery in her neck via intravenous. She was hooked up to a heart monitor that kept sounding its alarm. Doctors and nurses were repeatedly rushing to her side. Putting my trust in God, I prayed.

Both operations went well, and my daughter didn't require a colostomy bag. The doctors also straightened her nose and monitored her for any vision loss resulting from her fractured orbital socket. Seemingly on her way to a full recovery, two weeks later, she was transferred to our local hospital. When she was released a few months later, a nurse came to our home to change Mindy's abdominal dressings.

A year later, her back healed, the rod attached to Mindy's vertebrae was surgically removed. They had to remove the rod because the screws attaching it to her spine pressed against her flesh whenever she leaned her back on anything, making sitting uncomfortable. That surgery should have been the beginning of the end of Mindy needing pain medication. Instead, removing the rod was the onset of a nightmare that lasted for many years.

I'd been concerned about the amount of prescription pain killers they'd prescribed after my daughter's initial back surgery when she was fifteen years old. By the time she was twenty-one, she was on oxycodone and the slow-release version of the same medicine called Oxycontin. (Oxycodone is a semisynthetic opioid that is roughly 1.5 times more potent that morphine.) At the same time, she was also prescribed fentanyl patches. (Fentanyl is an opioid-based pain killer that is about 100 times more potent than morphine, 50 times more potent than heroine, and 400 times more potent than codeine.)

Mindy was prescribed 250 micrograms (mcgs) of fentanyl,

which consisted of two 100 mcg patches and one 50 mcg patch. The patches transdermally released opioids into her body over a three-day period. She had an allergic reaction to the adhesive. Whenever applying fresh patches, she had to search for areas of her skin that weren't already irritated and red.

My once socially active daughter who made friends wherever she went, was moody, irritable, and a recluse. Her body had become so dependent on prescribed narcotics that she lost all sense of her true self. She was a walking zombie riddled with depression and anxiety.

One night, extremely worried about Mindy's emotional state, her stepfather, sister and I took her to the hospital with the hope that they'd admit her to the psych ward and begin weaning her off the medications destroying her life. The Emergency doctor refused to admit her. When we threatened to sue him should Mindy die at home, he finally agreed to keep her for observation.

While she was in the hospital, we learned that the medical system wouldn't cover the $10,000 cost to place Mindy in a detox center. I couldn't believe my ears. The doctors who'd prescribed the potent mixture of narcotics were the ones responsible for my daughter's drug dependency. Whenever a doctor deemed that the effect of the medication had decreased, the dose was increased. Intelligent and wise, Mindy would never have even considered taking street drugs. It was grossly unfair that she had unwittingly become addicted to prescribed narcotics. How was it possible that the curative measure wasn't covered by the medical system?

Unable to afford the cost of placing Mindy in a detox center, she agreed to living with me and her stepfather while she gradually weaned off the drugs. To help us keep track of which medications she needed to take when, the pharmacist at our local drugstore blister-packed the pills. Rather than the usual four rows of daily medication most people take, Mindy's addictive assortment was packaged in eight rows.

To ensure she didn't detox too quickly, each week the pharmacist removed 5 mgs (milligrams) of Oxycontin and 5 mgs of oxycodone from one of the bubbles in the blister pack, slowly decreasing her blister pack from eight rows to three. As each row disappeared, the number of times she needed to daily take her medication decreased. Three times per day was far more reasonable.

To cope with the sweating, shaking and mood swings that accompanied each decrease, Mindy paced and ate chocolate. The amount of chocolate the girl ate would make most people throw up. But slowly, every month, the blister pack would lose a bubble, and I'd witness a layer of fog lift from my daughter's brain as a bit more light returned to her eyes.

With the support of her family and steadfast determination on her part, two long years later, the blister pack was gone. I was incredibly proud of her. Mindy had survived the constant physical and emotional upheaval of withdrawal. It was a bittersweet victory. Next, she had to wean off the fentanyl patches.

Having been there for my daughter while she withdrew from oxy did not prepare me for the rollercoaster through hell she endured as her fentanyl doses were gradually lowered. I never stopped praying for her as she shook violently, sweated profusely, and wept. After a couple of weeks, her body would stabilize, and she'd feel "normal" for a few days. Then she'd start stressing about the next reduction. Crying as I held her in my arms, she'd plead, "Mom, I can't do this anymore." My heart breaking, I'd calmly reassure her, "Yes, you can. I believe in you and I love you."

After one year of the evilness of withdrawing from fentanyl, Mindy was finally free of narcotics. I was elated, grateful and immeasurably impressed by my daughter's strength and courage. My prayers had been answered. Satan had left her body and my lovely daughter could again fully experience and enjoy her life. I kept telling her, "Your angels are with you and watching over you."

To celebrate her incredible victory, we decided to go on a family camping trip. Equally proud of and happy for Mindy, her older sister agreed to come with us. Our entire family would be together.

The weekend started out as one we'd all forever treasure. Listening to my daughters chatting and laughing as they rekindled their relationship warmed my heart. I'd prayed for this day for what seemed like forever. Mindy was happy, full of life and having a great time.

I was in our trailer getting ready for bed when I heard one of them scream, "Mom, Mom, Mom." When I opened the door, Mindy was crying and holding her elbow. I calmly asked her to come inside and helped her take off her hoody and shirt. Her hand was facing the wrong way.

Well retrieving trays of ice from the freezer, I asked her what had happened. She said that she'd tripped over and fallen into an unlit firepit on the beach. I placed the ice in a plastic bag and told her to hold it on her elbow while I went to get the car.

At Emergency, we learned that she had dislocated her elbow and fractured the peaks in the socket. As she'd been drinking, they couldn't sedate her. Instead, she was given a medication that made her eyes rapidly shift back and forth. The sound of her elbow being popped back into place sent shivers down my spine. Thankfully, Mindy reported that she felt nothing. We left the hospital with instructions to return the next day to see the orthopedic surgeon.

Following an operation on her elbow, despite Mindy's protest that she absolutely did not want to take narcotics, the surgeon insisted that she didn't have a choice. According to him, without drugs the pain would be unbearable, and her elbow wouldn't properly heal. And so began round three my daughter's nightmarish withdrawal from narcotics.

Witnessing her agony for a third time, I wondered why doctors so eagerly pushed narcotics. Did they get kickbacks from pharmaceutical companies? Didn't they care that long-term dependency on pain killers led to addiction? Were they oblivious to the suffering that accompanied withdrawal? Why did doctors and the medical system ignore how emotionally and physically taxing helping a loved one through withdrawal was for families? And what about people who didn't have a support system? Without being able to safely detox at a health center, those patients would forever be addicted, or suffer miserably as they fought their way through withdrawal, alone, sick and scared. It was a gross injustice perpetuated by a system of health professionals who'd taken an oath to heal, not harm, people.

It was two years before my daughter was again drug free. Determined to be her own advocate, she had her family doctor and specialists add "absolutely no narcotics" to her medical file.

Moving forward, life for my daughter was not easy. When the insurance claim from her car accident was settled, two men that she dated at different times took advantage of her financially before moving onto their next marks. Maybe because they'd found new interests that didn't include her, perhaps because they couldn't bear watching her suffer through withdrawal again, friends Mindy had once counted on, abandoned her. Despite what must have felt like betrayal after betrayal, Mindy didn't give up, she sought help.

A psychiatrist diagnosed her as having PTSD (post-traumatic stress disorder). She started attending church and made new friends. She found joy in her one-pound miniature terrier and in her relationships with her sister, stepdad and me. She again took pride in her surroundings, cleaning and decluttering the household mess that had accumulated during the years she'd been addicted. She took the beginner's test for her driving license but missed getting it by one wrong answer. With each step forward she took, I thought, "She's back. My beautiful, outgoing, capable daughter is back. Thank you, God."

When Mindy decided to travel to Ontario to visit her biological father, grandparents, uncles, aunts and numerous cousins, I was happy for her. Travelling by plane by herself was a gigantic step. While there, her half-sister's boyfriend introduced her to a guy Mindy found attractive and liked. Determined to continue concentrating on herself, she told him she wasn't ready for a serious relationship. She did, however, extend her holiday.

A few days before she left, her uncle's neighbor drugged and sexually assaulted Mindy. She reported the rape to the police, but as she was leaving the province and didn't wish to return for a trial, the monster wasn't charged. She came home visibly shaken and deeply depressed. Putting her faith in God, she resumed Bible study classes and reached out to a fellow student. She was determined to recover from the horrific incident and to continue on the path to God's holy light.

Not long after, while walking in broad daylight on her way to visit a friend, a man leaned out of his black van and asked Mindy for directions. When she walked closer to the van and stopped, he jumped out and tried to abduct her. Screaming, she punched and kicked him until she was able to break free. She ran the rest of the way to her friend's house and called the police. Two of her toes were broken and she was shaken to her core. After that incident, Mindy was afraid to leave her home alone. Still suffering with depression, except for when a family member took her shopping or to a doctor's appointment, she became a recluse.

Mindy stayed in touch with the guy she'd met through her half-sister in Ontario. He'd become her confidante and they chatted nearly every day. When he came for a visit, she was notably happier. It was obvious that she had strong feelings for him and felt safe when he was around. Aware of how sad she was when he left, I wasn't surprised when he asked her to move to Ontario.

Although she wanted to be with him, Mindy was hesitant about moving away from her family. When she asked what I thought, I encouraged her to take a chance and go. More than anything, I wanted my daughter to be happy. She left a few days after Christmas. Once there, she knew she'd made the right decision. When they got engaged, I was as thrilled as she was. Life had finally taken a positive turn for my girl.

My daughter and her fiancé made wonderful plans for their future. Unfortunately, Mindy became deathly ill with pneumonia (which happened almost every winter) and an obstructed bowel (which happened every few years as a result of the scar tissue that formed when she ruptured her bowel in the car accident). While she was hospitalized and too sick to protest, unaware of her history, the doctors gave her narcotics for the pain. A short while later, a gynecologist prescribed a medication that altered

Mindy's thinking and emotional well-being. In a state of mental emergency, she was hospitalized in a psych ward for three months.

When Mindy asked the doctor why he'd prescribed a medication that could alter her mental state, he apologized and explained that it was a rare reaction that affected less than two percent of those who took the drug. Standing up for herself, she told him that when you're one of those adversely affected, two percent was too high a risk to chance. I was pleased that she'd confronted the gynecologist. Although it was too late to prevent her suffering, by expressing her thoughts, she'd potentially helped other patients avoid a similar fate.

Unable to be by her side, I worried about Mindy night and day. When she and her fiancé decided that the best place for her to be was at home where her doctors knew her and could give her the best possible care, I was relieved. Still very much in love, they also decided that he would follow her to British Columbia, giving up his employment and leaving his family behind.

With the help of her family doctor, Mindy is in the process of withdrawing from narcotics a fourth time. She continues to seek help from mental health professionals and remains dedicated to her Bible studies. She and her fiancé have a nice home and she is starting to love herself again.

I am grateful that she has the courage and strength to carry on in spite of all she has endured. Whenever I mentioned this to her, Mindy reminds me that the angels surrounding her will continue to protect her.

Mindy's courage encourages me to be brave and bold in our mutual stance against medical professionals routinely prescribing narcotics to unwitting patients. It is grossly unfair that, like many others, my daughter endures the stigma of being labeled a drug addict because her body and mind became dependent on narcotics that doctors prescribed. Through sharing her story, we hope and pray that others will be spared the hellish nightmare of addiction and withdrawal.

Note: An addictive drug with analgesic and euphoric properties, accidental fentanyl overdoses by casual drug users is epidemic across North America. As heating the drug increases its potency, a high fever, sunbathing, and hot tubs increase the likelihood of an overdose. Fentanyl patches can cause serious or life-threatening breathing problems, especially during the first twenty-four to seventy-two hours. Side effects include headaches, mood changes, drowsiness, and depression.

About Brenda Flannery

Brenda Flannery and her husband, Robb, live in Courtenay on Vancouver Island in British Columbia. She has two daughters and two grandchildren who affectionately call her "Grams." An animal lover, she and Robb have a cat and two dogs she refers to as her *fur babies*.

Brenda has been in the health care field for twenty-five years and was a pharmacy technician for nine years. Currently, she is a Registered Care Aide (RCA) in a seniors' care facility and a manager with SendOutCards, a network marketing company.

Her medical knowledge continues to make Brenda a strong advocate for her loved ones when they are sick or injured. Her many talents include singing, composing songs, writing poetry, drawing and painting. When time permits, she and Robb hit the road in their motorhome. Feeling blessed, Brenda is grateful for the gifts inherent in every day.

Brenda published her daughter's story to encourage other parents to educate themselves about opioid dependency. Her daughter Mindy's hope is that reading her journey through addiction will help give others the courage, faith and strength needed to withdraw from prescribed painkillers and become their own medical advocates. Brenda and Mindy's combined message: rise above your adversities so that you can live the life you are meant to love.

Connect with Brenda Flannery
E-Mail: brenny1963@hotmail.com
Website: www.sendoutcards.com/flannery

Journey #4

CINDERELLA NO MORE

Charlene Janzen

Believing that I'd someday marry my Prince Charming, when I was young, every occasion was planned for our possible meeting. Getting ready to leave the house took hours as I ironed my clothes, showered, put on makeup, and styled my hair. When I was in my forties, I learned that to ensure that the two of us were never late for church or an appointment, when I lived with my parents, my mom would move the clock ahead by fifteen minutes without telling me.

Prince Mark arrived when I was eighteen. He was eight years older than me, wore a black trench coat, and seemed worldly and mysterious. A month after we met, he asked me to marry him. I excitedly accepted his proposal as visions of walking down the aisle wearing a flowing white dress danced in my mind. For the next few months, I lived on cloud nine as I asked my maid of honor and five bridesmaids to stand up with me, selected fancy invitations, ordered a tiered wedding cake, booked the church and minister, chose our wedding rings, and planned the meal that we would serve to the hundreds who'd attend the reception. We married in the summertime one year after we met.

My dream wedding went off without a hitch. I felt lucky, loved and adored by many. We slept in a hotel that night, which was fun until the sun came up and the glow of the wedding began to fade. Both of our families helped pay for our elaborate wedding. Paying for the honeymoon was up to Prince Mark and me.

Our savings limited, we decided to go camping at a nearby park in Collingwood, Ontario. The first and only night of our honeymoon, it rained buckets. Our tent flooded to the point that our air mattresses were floating. We gave up and slept in the car. Our marriage went downhill from there.

Within a few months, Prince Mark morphed into Mean Mark. Behind closed doors, he was physically abusive and often insulted and backhanded me. He forbade me from going out with friends and limited visits with my parents to once or twice a month. Every fight was my fault because I'd done or said something wrong. When I eventually shared what was happening with close friends, most said that they weren't surprised. Obviously, there'd been signs of Mark's controlling and abusive ways while we were dating. Too caught up in the planning of my fairy-tale wedding, I'd missed them all.

Fourteen months after we married, I told Mean Mark that our marriage was over. Soon after, I pawned my wedding ring and the small appliances and crystal serving dishes we'd received as wedding gifts, and purchased a one-way ticket to Vancouver, British Columbia. When I told Mom that I was moving three thousand miles away, she cried. But when I explained that I was afraid of Mark and wanted to get as far away as possible, she gave me her blessings.

I landed in Vancouver with eighty dollars in my pocket. Thankfully, a friend I'd met seven years earlier through a Christian youth group invited me to stay with him and his male roommates until I found a job and could afford my own place. As we had spent time together three or four times a year when he came to my hometown for a youth group function, I felt comfortable with the idea of living in the same house with the guys and him. I also wondered if we might start dating. It didn't take long for me to realize that at that point in his life, my friend wasn't ready to be anyone's Prince Charming.

Within a week of arriving in Vancouver, I found a job at a movie theater and a room to rent in a big house. The landlady who owned the house and rented me a small room in the attic seemed nice enough, but tenants weren't allowed to use the laundry facilities. About a week after I moved in, I called my ex-roommates to say hi. Richard, the roommate who'd rented the guys' house and the one who made sure the bills were paid, answered the phone. When I told him that I was planning to take a bus to a nearby laundromat, he offered to pick me up and let me do my laundry at the guys' house. When he arrived in his fancy white car with black leather bucket seats, it reminded me of Prince Charming transporting Cinderalla in his white horse-drawn carriage.

Richard was confident, smart and kind. He was taking a full course load at BCIT and working part-time at a brokerage company. It wasn't long before he became my boyfriend. On February 29th, five years after we started dating, I had a dozen red roses delivered to him at work where he was in charge of the computer department. The accompanying note said: "Will you marry me? Love, Charlene." When I hadn't heard from him by the afternoon, I called him to see if he'd received the flowers. He told me that he had. I asked him why he hadn't responded. He said, "We'll talk about it when I get home." My heart sank.

Later that evening, Richard explained that he wanted to be the one to propose. Although I told him I understood, I didn't. I felt rejected. A few months later in the summertime, we decided to visit his extended family in Nova Scotia. While our flight was taking off, Richard presented me with his mother's engagement ring from her first marriage and proposed. Excited, I said, "Yes!" Putting on the diamond-adorned ring, I assured him that if our relationship went south, I wouldn't pawn his mother's ring. When we were disembarking the plane, the flight attendants presented us with a bottle of champagne.

Neither of us wanted an elaborate wedding. We married in the fall of that year in front of a justice of peace at Minter Flower Garden in Chilliwack, B.C., which was an hour's drive out of the city. I paid seven dollars for my wedding dress: a purple formfitting knee-length velvet dress with white satin trim. Although our families knew we were getting married, we didn't invite any relatives. Two friends acted as our witnesses. Afterward, we honeymooned in Whistler, B.C. For three years we were best friends and blissfully happy.

A friend and I were on our way home from work when everything changed. Approaching an intersection, I noticed that the light had changed from red to green. I took my foot off the brake and pushed the gas pedal. A split second later, a large pickup truck crossed in front us, and we collided before I could hit the brake. The airbags employed and knocked me out for a few seconds. When I opened my eyes, the car was filled with smoke, my left arm was numb, and my wrist was the size of a football. My friend said her stomach hurt, but otherwise appeared uninjured. I used my right arm to open the driver's door to let out the smoke. When I did, a man asked if we were okay, assured us that the car wasn't on fire, and told us that it was safest for us to stay seated. After calling an ambulance, he called my friend's husband and then mine.

My friend's husband arrived before the ambulance. Richard showed up at the hospital forty-five minutes after he learned about the accident. When he arrived, I asked him what took him so long. His said that he had been dealing with the car. I was shocked and hurt. He was more concerned about the car than me. Rather than console me, he complained about being at the hospital.

Once home, he didn't offer to help me with anything before heading to his computer. Only able to use my right hand, I made soup for dinner and thought about our marriage and whether Richard would be a good father.

Every day after work, he played computer games from the second he entered our home until the wee hours of the morning. We seldom socialized together on weekends, and he no longer seemed interested in me. When I asked him to go to a marriage counselor, he refused. If he couldn't be there for me when I was injured, it wasn't likely that he'd be an attentive dad if we had children. As much as I wanted to be a mother, I had a choice to make. I could stay with Richard and not have kids...or leave him and hope that I'd one day meet a man who'd be a good father.

That night, I went to bed feeling hopeless and heartbroken. Four weeks and numerous relationship disappointments later, I rented a basement suite in a coworker's home, and left my husband. Having twice failed at love, I wondered: *Did I expect too much from men? Was I destined to be single and childless? Would I ever meet an authentic Prince Charming?*

Having always loved singing, a few months later, I decided to try karaoke. Although my hands trembled with fear, I was hooked from the first song. For the next few weeks, I went to karaoke a couple of times a week and practiced in my living room every chance I could. When Vic Pearce's family band asked me to sing with them at a local branch of the Royal Canadian Legion, I thought I'd made it to the big time. Unfortunately, unnerved by the idea of singing with a band, the sound tech had to keep turning up the microphone because I was singing so softly.

Karaoke folks are a friendly bunch. Over the next year, I sang in various establishments and met numerous musically-minded souls including the members of The Backstage Club. Wanting to help further my career and knowing that I was far less than rich, a friend sold me a guitar for $300 that he claimed was old and used. The case was worn; the guitar was new. It was a wonderful gesture. When fans started following my show, I was flattered. Having the time of my life, I stayed single for several months.

When I was sixteen-years-old, I went to New York City on a school trip. While exiting a Broadway show, I tripped on a step and started to fall. Someone caught me. When I looked up to thank the person, I was speechless. The man had the most gorgeous grey-blue eyes I'd ever seen. "May I get you a limo?" he asked. "No, thank you," I said. "I have a limo waiting for me." Walking way, I chuckled. My limo was a Greyhound bus.

Years later, when a new manager started at the insurance company where I worked, I noticed him. He had beautiful crystal-clear blue eyes, was confident, and physically fit. Like the man who'd caught me mid-flight on the stairs in New York, I felt an instant connection with him. Through conversation, I learned that he had travelled the world. As he continually flirted with me, it seemed that he was equally attracted to me. But he never asked me out. After I learned that he'd sung my praises to my supervisor, I sent him a thank you card and asked him out for coffee. His response was not what I expected.

He set up a formal meeting, and said, "I can't say it wouldn't happen or can't happen. But at this point in time, I can't have coffee with you." I was confused, embarrassed and hurt. Unable to endure the humiliation of continually interacting him, I asked to be transferred to another insurance center, which I was. He was out of sight, but he was never out of mind. I thought about him night and day, often wondering if he was my true soul mate.

A few months later, I was asked to be the master of ceremonies for the head office Christmas party. As part of being the emcee, I was asked to write and sing a song about the company. I composed a song and set it to the tune of "YMCA" by The Village People. During the chorus when the three hundred employees in attendance started mimicking the alphabet letters I formed with my arms, I was proud and happy. Secretly hoping that the manager from my previous office would attend the party, I was crushed when he didn't show.

In January 2003, I met Rob. He seemed nervous and nice. According to him, we'd been introduced a year early. Apparently when I sang "La Isla Bonita" by Madonna, he decided to ask me for a date. Before I agreed to go out with him, I asked him if he went to church. Both of my ex-husbands were nonbelievers, and I'd decided that the next man I dated would be a churchgoer, like me. Rob said he regularly attended church, and we arranged to meet at a restaurant the next Sunday following the service at our respective churches.

I arrived an hour late for our date and was impressed that Rob waited for me without getting angry. During dinner, I learned that he travelled for work, was close to his family, and enjoyed spending time with his nieces and nephew. He seemed incredibly kind, so when he asked if I wanted to go out with him a second time, I said, "Yes!"

We started dating. For Valentine's Day, Rob took me for a weekend ski trip to Sun Peaks Resort in Kamloops, British

Columbia. In March, to celebrate my birthday, he took me to the Kamloops Cowboy Festival. When we returned home, he gave me a beautiful brown suede jacket with fringe and rhinestones. When I put on the jacket and looked in the mirror, I thought, "If I were a country star, this would be the perfect jacket for stepping off a tour bus to greet a crowd of adoring fans." As we'd talked about getting married and Rob's gift was expensive, for me, the multitude of rhinestones represented an engagement ring.

In May, Rob secured a government job in Winnipeg, Manitoba. He was happy that he wouldn't have to travel as much as he had with his previous job and asked me to relocate with him. Not wild about leaving my home near Vancouver, B.C., I was torn. After he moved, I prayed and did a lot of soul searching.

One day while walking on the beach, I asked God to help me make the right decision. When I returned to my car and put on the radio, the first song I heard was "Man! I Feel Like a Woman!" by Shania Twain. Recalling the numerous times that we'd sung that song together and how everyone laughed whenever I stopped singing and Rob sang the words *man, I feel like a woman*, I smiled. I knew then that I had to go to Winnipeg. My guardian angels had given me the sign I needed.

Within a few weeks, Rob came to Vancouver to help me move my furniture to Winnipeg. Nervous and excited when I met him at the airport, I body checked him, grabbed his bag, threw it in the backseat, jumped in the front seat and started the car. "Wait! Wait!" Rob said as I put the car in reverse. "I have something to ask you." Fairly certain I knew what he was going to ask, my heart skipped a few beats as I put the car in park. Rob presented me with a beautiful engagement ring with a solitaire diamond in the center and a smaller diamond on either side. "I knew it!" I said. "Yes!" Even though I never gave him the opportunity to do so, I teasingly gave him heck for not getting down on one knee to propose.

The night before we left, I was asked to audition for a band. As we hadn't finished packing the moving truck, I couldn't. About a thousand miles into the drive to Winnipeg, worried about whether I'd made the right decision, I had a panic attack. I had given up my job, apartment, car, and a chance to sing in a band. Without getting upset, Rob pulled the truck to the side of road and offered to drive me back to Vancouver. Thinking that his gesture was one of the sweetest things anyone had ever offered to do for me, I said, "Let's keep going."

Although I felt isolated and alone in Winnipeg, with Rob's encouragement, I started singing karaoke at local bars and entered a singing contest sponsored by a country radio station. Out of sixty contestants, I came sixth and was proud when my name was announced on the radio. The top ten singers were then asked to perform at a bar for an elimination round. The first contestant to be eliminated, I was disheartened, but agreed to perform again on the final night of the contest. Rebellious by nature, rather than sing a country song, I sang the rock 'n' roll song "Hit Me with Your Best Shot" by Pat Benatar. There forward, whenever I sang in a country music radio contest, the host would say, "Now, Charlene. You have to sing country tonight."

Nine months after we started dating, Rob and I decided to fly from Manitoba to British Columbia to get married. Rob paid for their flights from Ontario so that my mom, dad, brother, sister-in-law and nephew could attend our wedding.

On the big day, I had a massage, steam shower and then a mud bath. While showering off the mud, I became lightheaded and sat on the floor. Unable to walk, without caring that I was naked, I crawled to the door and hollered for help. A few friends came to my rescue, covered me with a towel, called 911 and then Rob. After explaining that my blood pressure had plummeted, the ambulance attendants advised me to go to the hospital. Determined to go ahead with the wedding and our honeymoon, I reassured everyone that I was fine and didn't need to be checked out further.

We were married in a tiny church with one hundred people in attendance. Following our candlelight wedding ceremony, we moved to a hotel for the reception. We all danced and a few of us took turns singing karaoke. It was after midnight when Rob and I went to bed in the penthouse suite. A few hours later, we headed for the airport.

Rob planned our honeymoon. I had no idea where we were going. While going through airport security in the United States, a guard said, "So, you are going to San Juan, Puerto Rico." I said, "We are?!" Seemingly alarmed, the security guard took a step toward Rob. "It's okay," I hurriedly explained. "We're on our honeymoon and our final destination was supposed to be a surprise for me." Just before our final flight landed, Rob handed me a brochure highlighting the ports we'd visit on the Caribbean cruise we were about to take. It was a dream come true for me.

Ten years after we were married, Rob and I and our two daughters took a road trip to British Columbia. While in Vancouver, we visited a friend in the hospital. As we were leaving, I spotted the manager who'd rejected my coffee invitation. Our eyes locked, and my heart starting thumping. He was talking on the phone and started walking towards us as he said, "There she is, and she has two cute girls with her." I freaked. It was intense, too intense. I grabbed my kids' hands, mumbled something about taking them potty, and hurried away. As we walked by him, he said, "She doesn't recognize me without my goatee." When we came out of the bathroom he was gone.

Consumed with the idea that my ex-manager was my true Prince Charming and I'd let him get away, I couldn't sleep for over a week. I was admitted to the hospital for exhaustion. While there, I was diagnosed as being bipolar. Determined to get home to my family as quickly as possible, I thought about the various men in my life and why I felt I needed to be rescued.

My father was a farmer who worked long hours. When I was young, the only time I saw Dad was late at night when I got out of bed to spend a few minutes with him. I didn't have a meaningful relationship with him until I moved to British Columbia and we started chatting over the phone. Through our conversations, I came to understand that Dad hadn't chosen to ignore me when I was a child, he was doing his best to be a good provider. The day that we finally said I love you to each other was a big step for both of us. We have remained close since.

My first husband was eight years older than me. I didn't need a psychology degree to know why I'd married him when I was only eighteen. He was a father substitute. Unlike my actual Dad, however, he was abusive, not kind. Although my second husband was a good man, his lack of caring for me when I was in the car accident led me to realize that he wouldn't be a hundred percent available to any children we might have. Having felt like I didn't have a dad when I was a child, finding an attentive father for my children was paramount for me. *Why then did I still feel the need to be rescued by a Prince Charming when my current husband was wonderful to my children and me?*

The answer was that I was looking for romantic perfection. As a young girl, I'd naively bought into the idea of soul mates that were destined to meet and live happily ever after. As an adult, part of me still believed that it was possible to sustain the idealism depicted in fairy tales, television shows and movies. What I hadn't thought through was that all romance stories conclude when the princess and her shining knight get married.

Cinderella may have married the prince and moved to the castle, but what then? Surely, rather than personally caring for her every whim, her husband would have left the fulfilling of the princess's and their children's needs up to numerous chambermaids, cooks and servants. Past their physical attraction to each other, what did the prince and Cinderella have in common? What would they talk about? Laugh about? Cry about? If their relationship was built on physical attraction, wouldn't they fall out of love as the years robbed them of youth? The more I pondered romantic idealism, the sillier it seemed. But not entirely.

My romantic notions had inspired me to keep searching until I'd found the perfect husband for me and our two daughters. When I met Rob, I knew that he would one day make a great father. Time and time again, he has proven me right.

When our youngest started having seizures, Rob became a scout leader so that he could be by her side. He takes one of our daughters sailing while enjoying sword-fighting and archery with the other. As both of us enjoy having lots of children in our home, we also host teenagers from other countries who want to study in Canada.

Rob is a selfless, caring and loving man who always puts our family first. One Valentine's Day, he and our girls decorated the dining room with flowers, candles, and garland on the walls. He also bought pizza and a movie for the girls and set them up in the living room. Once the girls were settled, Rob presented me with my favorite meal, shrimp fettucine, which he'd made. It was a wonderfully romantic evening complete with soft music playing in the background. He truly is a great father and a wonderful husband.

Our sixteen-year marriage has not always been a bed of rose petals. There are thorny times when I need to draw on a visualization exercise that I came up with when I was hospitalized. Closing my eyes, I envision a light switch. At the top of the light switch is the word "positive" and at the bottom is the word "negative." Whenever I feel down or overwhelmed, I imagine flipping the light switch to "positive" and using duct tape to secure it in position. This simple imagining helps me to stay positive no matter what.

Together, Rob and I have endured the ups and downs of my bipolar disorder. He often jokes that to get rid of him, I will have to kneecap him. Whenever I admit that I don't give him enough credit for sticking by my side, he agrees that I don't. All kidding aside, I am happy and content. Rob and I, our daughters and the teens we host are a family in every sense of the word. We may not always live a fairy-tale existence, but when things go awry, we've got imaginary duct tape, our commitment to one another, and an abundance of love to keep us strong and moving forward in a positive direction.

About Charlene Janzen

Charlene Janzen, her husband, Rob, and their daughters live in Comox, British Columbia. Charlene is working toward a Bachelor of Arts degree with a major in English. Having married her Prince Charming, her plan is to publish a series of romance novels.

In addition to writing and spending time with family and friends, Charlene enjoys painting and reading. Ever-supportive, Rob accompanies her to karaoke gigs whenever possible.

Connect with Charlene Janzen
E-Mail: cjcreations@thejanzenhouse.com
Facebook: www.facebook.com/charlene.janzen.5

Journey #5

AN EVER-EVOLVING WISER MAN

Gerry Beazely

As I dialed Marilyn's number, I imagined her expecting my call. Her house would likely be quiet except for soft music playing in the background. Mondays were a time for her to reflect on events of the weekend and the healing energy she'd helped others tune into and utilize. I was one of her newest Reiki (pronounced ray-key) students and had recently completed her level one training.

"Hello," she said quietly.

"Good morning, Master. This is Gerry."

"And what can I do for you this morning?" she asked, not a hint of surprise in her voice. It wasn't the first time I'd called with questions.

"I could hardly sleep last night and my whole body tingles. What can I do about that?"

"In class, I explained that your Reiki attunement would change the way your system deals with and handles universal energy. It takes everyone a while to process the information and learn how to handle the energy."

"But I can't touch anything without getting a spark! Is that normal?" I persisted.

"Gerry, Gerry, Gerry." Marilyn's laugh bordered on a giggle. "I told you things would be different and that your natural energy would *react to* and *interact with* everything around you. Get used to it. It will never go away, and there isn't an off switch."

"I can't even touch my head because my hands are so hot.

And my hugs seem almost painful to most everyone."

"That's because your own energy is strong. Be patient. It will take time for you to learn how to control it, but it will be worth it when you can. Relax and meditate for a while. Call me tomorrow."

After thanking Marilyn for taking time to talk with me, I reflected on my journey into the world of Reiki.

Introduction to Reiki

I was introduced to energy healing through another patient's practitioner when Sharron, my late wife, was in the hospital being treated for her long-suffered and severe COPD (chronic obstructive pulmonary disease). After hearing a description of what Reiki entailed, Sharron shocked me by saying, "That is the same kind of treatments you have been giving me for years." Apparently, she was referring to the many times I was able to help her to calm her system and be comfortable when she was in pain and agitated from being unable to breathe properly. When Sharron learned that the Reiki master/practitioner had invited me to a Mother Mary's Healing Circle meeting, she insisted I go.

That Sunday after the meeting, I was approached by a lovely woman named Rochelle who kindly offered to give me a Reiki "healing," which I graciously and curiously accepted. Once I was comfortably seated in a chair, Rochelle stood behind me, took a deep breath and exhaled slowly. Silent except for her breathing, I easily sensed her physical movements and the energy emanating through her hands. Although she didn't touch me, I felt warmth on my head, across my shoulders, down my arms and back, and then on my head and shoulders again as she concentrated the energy.

As I wrote about in my chapter, "Coming of Age," in *Earth*

Angels #1, during that healing session, in my mind's eye, I saw what resembled a distant nebula with rainbows of color emanating from the center and expanding outward. Soft chanting played in my head as beautiful hues of reds, oranges, yellows, greens, blues, and golden-flecked purples continually burst into kaleidoscopic patterns that undulated with the rhythm of the chanting. Throughout the session, I felt loved and safe, much like I did when I was a young boy and my grandmother would wrap me in her arms as I sat on her lap. Then, without warning, the rest of the world stopped for me as my body and the chair seemingly rose in the air, moved to the right, plunked down harshly on the floor, and just as shockingly, flung back into place.

Still standing behind me, Rochelle softly said, "There you are. You should feel better now." I wasn't speechless but certainly at a loss for words. After we hugged, she left me alone to process a truly surreal experience.

When I shared my experience with Sharron, she encouraged me to develop what she saw as my innate healing abilities. Ten days later, on June 22, 2010, she succumbed to the COPD that had caused her incredible pain and aggravation. In spite of telling myself I was prepared for her passing and had steeled myself for the inevitable, the impact of losing my twin flame/soul mate and best friend shattered my existence into a sad and foreign reality.

As a way of coping, I submerged myself in hours of research on the Internet, learning everything I could about Reiki and other metaphysical modalities. I also attended Mother Mary's Healing Circle meetings and joined two educational circles. The friends I made accepted my mix of grief and joyful personal growth as I embarked on the path Sharron had encouraged me to follow. Kind of herding me whenever I lost my way, I will forever be grateful for Jean and Ted who became closer friends and my saviors.

Level One Reiki Training

Marilyn's class began at 10:00 a.m. and was intense throughout the day. She began by introducing the small group of us to the overall concept and intricacies of energy healing. Following a light lunch, she guided us through a meditation where we experienced an "attunement" with universal energy. Wow! Following the meditation, we were encouraged to share our perceptions.

I was strangely nervous as I listened to those who shared before me. Filled with self-doubt, a series of questions came to mind as I tried to rationalize my experience. That didn't happen for me, I wonder why. What if my attunement didn't work? My whole body is buzzing with a weird vibration. How come no one else mentioned being able to literally feel the energy? Why would I have such a different experience than the others in the class? I'm older than any of the others, chronologically speaking, so maybe that makes me different. I am the only male in the class. I really don't know much about metaphysical phenomena, maybe I just don't understand what happened. Did I really see an insanely large gold-scaled dragon? Maybe Marilyn hypnotized me again. Am I the comic relief for the day? Have I got the nerve to tell the others about my meditation experience? I think not! When Marilyn asks me to share, I will just pass. I don't want people to think I'm nuts. Am I nuts?

Despite my reservations, when Marilyn asked me to share, I gathered my courage and described my experience during the attunement meditation. Everyone listened intently. Their keen interest helped me to ground in the reality of my experience and to welcome their thoughts and comments. Everyone was kind and encouraging. No one suggested that I'd lost my mind.

Following another short break, my classmates and I practiced giving and receiving the healing energy of Reiki on one another. By the end of the day, I was anxious to gallop along my new life path.

Practice Makes Perfect, Or Not

As I began to reach out to friends and family to find my personal Reiki guinea pigs, many surprises came my way. The most dramatic lesson learned was that my extremely religious family, following my mother's lead, firmly believed that energy healing was not an acceptable practice. Somehow, never fully explained to me, it violated one or more of the points of doctrine which they followed. Some of their friends, however, were anxious to take advantage of my services. "Treating" one of them at a church luncheon almost got me burned at the stake.

My sister's friend, a most willing target of my new talents, was obviously in great pain. Upon hearing of my level one class, he immediately asked for my help. While I worked on him for about twenty minutes, I was totally unaware of the comments of the church community around us. When the fanatical zealots became loud enough to penetrate my focus, I responded in kind. Some of them abruptly left the room after expressing deep concern that my actions were not sanctioned by *powers that be*, whoever *they* may be.

Those in the family who recognized the value of Reiki seemed to expect actual miracles and failed to realize I was a student and they were my "lab animals," so to speak. It amazed me that these folks were willing to embrace the idea of energy healing, but only in the context of their strongly implanted religious doctrines.

Fortunately, a few friends became my clients and have enjoyed the benefits of Reiki since. The husband and wife of one such couple were at opposite ends of the belief-spectrum in the beginning. While I worked what he called "voodoo" on his wife, the husband expressed his distain even though he could see the physical benefits as changes occurred. Almost a year after I started working on his wife, he had an accident and severely injured his shoulder. He was obviously in a great deal of pain but claimed he had it under control.

In Reiki level one training, we were advised not to work on someone without consent. While not forbidding it, the alternative was to have your spiritual guides ask the person's guides for permission. With this backdoor exception in mind, one evening while he was asleep in his favorite chair, after getting instant approval from our respective guides, I performed Reiki on him for about twenty minutes. When he awakened, he stood, shrugged and wandered off to the washroom. Upon his return, he walked directly to where I was seated.

"You did that without my permission," he sternly accused.

"I asked my guides to ask yours and they said it was okay," I replied glibly.

"I will have to have a word with them," he barked before softening his tone. "I must admit that my shoulder does feel a great deal better. You'd better get your beauty sleep and be full of energy for the next while, because you'll be working on me regularly as well." What a boost to my self-confidence.

Shortly after that exchange, I was asked to become a part of a "closed" educational meditation group. My surprised and thrilled response may have been heard clearly from coast to coast. The host and the facilitator both had impressive credentials and reputations, and I was grateful for the opportunity to learn from those with such intense and varied experience.

The attendees were also a surprise. Two of the ladies were

friends of mine. Another was a young woman I'd hired for her first job when I was a manager at a Wendy's restaurant. Almost every Monday following our meditation meeting, a small group of us met for coffee at a nearby Tim Hortons. Depending on what we'd covered during the educational portion of our meeting and the alternate conversational routes that inspired, we often chatted to three in the morning or later.

Shortly after being invited to join the first, I was invited to participate in another educational meditation group facilitated by a strong and unique woman who became a mentor, Theresa Dupuis. Almost everything outside of my new path seemed unimportant as I focused my efforts on an array of fascinating metaphysical modalities. Unfortunately, redirecting my interests and attention came with blessings and consequences.

My late wife and I had a manufacturing/distribution business, which we successfully grew and managed for twenty-five years. When she became too ill to work, we transferred part ownership and the day-to-day management of the business to two younger family members. They couldn't get along well enough to make a cup of coffee.

Slightly more than one year after Sharron's passing, the company no longer existed. Every aspect of the business reminded me of Sharron, making it difficult to concentrate whenever I was asked and/or tried to help. Broke, sad and disheartened, in June 2011, I declared personal bankruptcy. Thankfully, the friends I'd made through Reiki and the two meditation groups supported me through what was truly a desperate time in my life.

Educational Meditation Groups

When Marilyn announced the date of her next level two Reiki training, I instantly asked to be included. I was disappointed when she refused my request with the explanation that I had not yet completely resolved my issues with level one. Committed to learning what I needed to know to overcome this hurdle, I attended every spiritual healing and psychic event that occurred in the Fraser Valley and Greater Vancouver areas. I also continued participating in the two educational meditation groups.

The first group focused on a variety of subjects including the development of one's mediumship and physic abilities. The meditations were guided by the facilitator. One memorable meditation took me down a path in a beautiful valley of grassy fields and trees. As I walked, I noted a particularly large tree in close relationship to the path. Seeing the outline of a door in the bark, I diverted to investigate. After easily opening the door, I entered a large area that resembled a tesseract (four-dimensional) building. Directly ahead of me was a maze-like area that reminded me of pictures I'd seen of castle mazes in the United Kingdom and Europe.

I vaguely noted the outer door closing as I moved toward and entered the maze. Within, there were shrubs and trees of such bright and varied colors that I found it hard to focus on any one part for more than a few seconds. Directly before me was a purple hedge, which had been carved into the shape of a reptile similar to an alligator. When I stopped to admire it, the hedge became a life-like alligator with its jaws opened widely to expose rows of teeth that could easily chomp a person in half. Then its jaws closed as the alligator became as gentle as a puppy and allowed me to pet and stroke it. When I stroked its head, it disappeared as various scenes flashed before me. Some I interpreted as probable past lives, some appeared to represent my current life, and others seemed to be glimpses of my future.

Within a few minutes, I noticed light reflecting off the golden scales of the dragon I'd seen during a level one Reiki meditation. I'd known my guide was large, but was surprised to see that its eyes were the size of dinner plates and a shiny deep red. Its body language was gentle and the slight flame that belched with each exhalation of breath was just plain cute. I was totally enamored.

Focusing my attention on the impressive golden beast redirected my attention to the scenes of future events that continued to flash by. In one vision, I saw myself reading cards for an indistinguishable person. In another, I was doing mediumship in front of a large, crowded room. Each of these visions represented a goal of my development and were easily interpreted.

Visions of my past lives, however, were unexpected and profound. In a previous life, I saw myself as a Mayan priest preparing for a solstice ceremony high in the mountains. In another, I viewed a Tibetan monastery high in the mountains where I was the Khenpo or abbot, part of whose job was the supervision of an enormous travel vortex that was part of the monastery. In a third previous life, I was a first dynasty Egyptian priest wearing a gold-trimmed black robe as I stood in what appeared to be a storeroom.

The second educational meditation group facilitated by Theresa was equally fascinating. As a small group of us meditated, in a soft voice, she would lead us to a common area in the universe that encouraged us to explore higher planes of existence and astral travel. After an appropriate time, during which she noted her observations of each member of the group, she would "call" us back. Frequently, she asked one member of the group to "stay" where they had travelled. After the other group members were safely back, she'd give us small flashlights and have us shine the beam on the person still travelling. Theresa would then question the person still travelling about what they could see. Her questions included specifics about the general surroundings, inhabitants, architecture, transportation systems, and any other details that arose from her initial enquiries. She would also ask the traveler to check his/her footwear and whether he/she was an observer or had taken on the character of a local.

The unique experiences described by travelers were enthralling. On occasion, I was asked to stay where I'd traveled. From my description of one place I frequently visited, Theresa dubbed the inhabitants "ant people." A highly developed civilization of beings whose upper and lower torsos were connected by a narrow waist similar to the petiole connecting the thorax and abdomen of earth ants, the beings walked upright, were notably graceful and extraordinarily tall. The average height of adults was about seven feet. Newborns were three feet tall and immediately learned to walk on two legs. The spectacular architecture looked like playground monkey bars on the outside. The extremely active inhabitants easily climbed to their residences on top. Ground transportation consisted of antigravity vehicles. Air transportation was also evident; however, I was not able to spend enough time to access it. When I initially visited the ant people, I was in human form and excitedly welcomed. During subsequent visits, I was encouraged to be a "walk in" where I actually shared a body with a local inhabitant and became part of their civilization. Although I thoroughly enjoyed my experiences with the ant people, I was always happy to return to my own body on earth.

Level Two Reiki

As it turned out, Marilyn's insistence that I wait to take her level two Reiki course was a godsend. With intention and practice, I gradually learned how to harness the energy emanating from spirit through me. When I did, my relationship with the healing properties of Reiki magnified.

Level two Reiki opened doors in my brain beyond its previous scope of understanding, and my new path became much clearer and more demanding. Some concepts of universal energy we studied were easy to comprehend and mentally digest. Others had me doing research on the Internet for hours on end. Gratefully, all propelled me further along my spiritual path.

I particularly enjoyed learning about crystals and auras. It fascinated me that crystals absorb and emit the healing energies of spirit and that auras reflect the energy of the physical and etheric bodies.

During the meditation sessions, I uncovered more about who I had been in past lives and who I was at the core of my current being. These striking forays into astral and higher plane levels of travel were extraordinary in every way. One experience that stands out for me was revisiting a past life I'd glimpsed during level one training—I was once a priest of Isis in the first dynasty of Egypt assisting the household members of a priestess who had passed to join her in the afterlife.

Following our meditation and level two attunement, my classmates and I practiced Reiki on one another and on Marilyn. At the completion of training, we left with the master's blessing to continue our learning and development through our efforts as practitioners.

That fall at a psychic fair operated by Theresa, she introduced me to a young friend of hers, Dr. Steve Tyers. The fair was part of larger wellness show and I was one of the Reiki practitioners. Well we chatted, Steve explained how science and metaphysics fit hand in glove. He also told me that devices were being developed that would improve our understanding of energy healing and make our efforts more comprehensible for clients. The end result would be better and quicker healing for our clients. Steve's enthusiasm rubbed off on me. Before he left that day, we worked together on two clients. I learned new techniques, upped my personal understanding of energy healing, and solidified a deep and lasting friendship.

Reiki Master Attunement

In November 2011, I was graced with attunement to the level of Reiki Master. Attaining a master-level understanding of the relationships between universal energy, crystals and spiritual connections was a huge deal for me. I was feeling elated as we sat around a table and recounted our experiences during the meditation and attunement. As our discussion was ending, I noticed that one of my classmates, a medium, was being unusually quiet. When I asked her if anything was bothering her, she said there was a man with her who wanted to talk to me. When I asked her who it was, she said that he claimed to be my father.

As my father and I had not parted on great terms prior to his passing, I wasn't interested in hosting more of his hijinks some thirty-three years later. When he pressed the medium for my attention, I made communicating with him conditional on his proving who he was. If he could provide my friend with an accurate description of where I'd spent my formative years, including with whom, I would grant him an audience. I was still very ho-hum about the mediumship business, so my test was meant to satisfy me on that count as well.

I could not believe my ears when the medium described my childhood home in great detail (some of which I had forgotten) and provided perfect descriptions of my grandparents. Aghast, I agreed to hear what my father had to say. His message was that he was sorry for the way he had acted towards me regarding his church and his "ministries." He was especially sorry for how he'd behaved during times when he had met my then employers. When he asked for my forgiveness, I told him I would think about it and let him know.

Roughly two weeks later when I "felt" him around me for the umpteenth time, I forgave him. When I did, it lightened my state of mind regarding my family and my relationship with my father.

Teaching Reiki

As excited as I was about achieving the level of Reiki Master, the opportunity to teach caused me some concern. For the next while, I continued to attend the educational circles and a weekly metaphysical night at one of the local coffee shops where they usually had to ask us to leave at closing time. I also took on a larger role in our bi-weekly healing circle. In 2012, I finally felt ready to start teaching Reiki. It was a little scary to begin with, but I quickly learned to love the experience.

Reiki practitioners are advised to use the energy available from the universe and Mother Earth to promote healing in one's clients. Using your own personal energy during "healing" events is discouraged because it rapidly exhausts the practitioner. Teaching is different. During class, a Reiki teacher will often use his/her own energy. Provided a teacher has mastered the art of using and preserving one's energy, he/she will have enough energy to last throughout the day. However, using one's personal energy usually requires a one or two day recovery period, depending on how many students were in the class.

Throughout my many years of teaching, I've discovered that some students are more adept at mastering the intricacies of Reiki than others. Those that need more of my focus remind me of my daily calls to Marilyn following my level one training. Regardless of their skill level, my efforts are always to provide students with experiences similar to the ones I've enjoyed. I adore all my students and sometimes worry that I haven't given them enough, which is one of two reasons they are always invited to audit future classes. The other reason—I want to see them again!

* * *

When I think back over the years, I often recall my initial experience with Reiki. The beauty I pictured in my mind's eye, my sense of peace, and my awe at the abrupt movement at the end of my first "treatment." My sense of joy and wonder regarding Reiki could easily be wrapped up in Rochelle's final words that fateful day: "There you are. You should feel better now."

I feel blessed to have enjoyed numerous meaningful relationships with friends I've met through Reiki. My friendship with Nik, an older gentleman I met at my first Mother Mary's Healing Circle, is one I will forever treasure. When I entered and surveyed the room, my eyes settled on him. Seated next to Theresa, he was obviously not in the best of health, but the sparkle in his eyes told me that he was enjoying himself immensely.

When our eyes met, he seemed amused by what he saw and winked at me. Thinking that I knew he'd wink, I winked back. After the meeting we chatted. Nik had led an interesting life. He'd been in WW II and his best friend had been killed next to him just prior to the end of the war. While he recounted stories, I could picture whatever event he was recalling, sometimes adding details or finishing a story. He would then confirm whatever I'd said. He left shortly after the meeting with a promise to talk again.

Our reunion was not what either of us expected. The next time I saw him was when a few of us gathered around his bed in his daughter's home. As though his skin were transparent, I could see the human energy meridian system in his body. Nik passed that day. The last thing he said to me was whispered in my ear: "Get out there and heal the world."

Spurred on by a question I was asked by a near stranger, my interest in past lives continues. After telling me that I'm currently in my 94th iteration on earth, he asked, "Why are you still here when you are fully evolved?" In that moment, I had no idea how to respond. Upon reflection, the answer came to me. I'm here to explore life's endless opportunities. I'm here to celebrate my own and others' growth, successes and accomplishments as we each progress along our respective paths. I'm here for the ride! *Oh, what a ride life can be!*

About Gerry Beazely

Gerry Beazely (most often referred to as G) lives in Maple Ridge, British Columbia. He is a Reiki master teacher/practitioner, a crystal therapy teacher/practitioner, an intuitive spiritual counselor/coach and a medium. Gerry is also the owner of Natural Energy Wellness Centre.

A thoughtful and reflective person, G has been described as possessing the warmth of a Santa Claus and the zenful wisdom of a guru. An advocate for the arts and causes he holds dear, he is actively involved in the community. G enjoys golf, swimming, photography, karaoke, and lapidary work.

Semiretired, G is busier than he was when he and his late wife, Sharron, ran a thriving art stamp business. When he isn't traveling to showcase healing gemstones and crystal items at trade fairs, his weekends are spent at Fraser Valley farm markets where he sells honey for Golden Meadows Honey Farm.

A gifted writer with an enviable sense of humor, G is working on a series of short stories about living, loving and laughing. His chapter, "Coming of Age, in *Earth Angels #1*, is a wonder-filled account of his childhood, marriage and eventual foray into the metaphysical realm. Age sixty-four when he finally realized the truths in his Grandma Helen's spiritual teachings, G couldn't help but wonder whether his dying wife's selfless predictions would prove to be true too. Perhaps the answer would be revealed late at night when his grandfather's spirit visited him again.

Connect with G (Gerry) Beazely
E-Mail: ReikiMasterG@gmail.com
Facebook: www.facebook.com/gerry.beazely
Website: www.facebook.com/NaturalEnergyWellnessCentre

Journey #6

THIS ACORN DIDN'T FALL FAR FROM THE TREE

Jennie Potter

Dad, when you were just an acorn, you fought hard for the light and water to grow. Your roots began in Africa. Born and raised in Kenya, you spent your formative years in boarding schools, experienced wealth, and then lost when everything was taken away due to a family tragedy.

In your school days, the teachers beat you for wrong answers on tests, literally standing over you with a stick as you wrote. You ran miles to evade school bullies and became one of the fastest runners in your school. A natural entrepreneur and opportunity creator, you sold candy to kids in the schoolyard, saved a small fortune, and selflessly gave money to family when it was needed. Every day, every year, you fought and found light to grow.

When you left school, with fire in your belly and nothing to lose, you joined the army and became an elite paratrooper. When you set eyes on Mom, you knew she was the one. As the story goes, you asked her out every day for weeks, until finally, out of sheer exasperation, she said yes. On that first date, you said, "You are the woman I am going to marry."

Just as you pursued Mom, you went after all your dreams relentlessly. I'm not sure you ever took "no" for an answer. Mom finally said yes to your marriage proposal, and the two of you moved to Canada. Shortly after, you married in the small town of Dryden, Ontario, where you landed briefly before moving further west for opportunity. There you put down another root, and the sapling continued to grow.

In Edmonton, Alberta, you and Mom created more opportunities. While you went to flying school, proficient at shorthand and multitasking, Mom worked as a secretary to help make ends meet. The two of you lived on canned potatoes and made do with wooden crates for furniture. One of your first jobs was flying in the bush. Mom, straight out of London, complete with go-go boots and trendy hair, was often alone in the company-owned log cabin for days. Together, you made it work.

You wanted a better life, and you made it happen through sheer determination. When no one in the airline business was hiring, you went to the main commercial airline's head office, and asked to speak with the man in charge. When the secretary said he wasn't available, you said you'd wait. The secretary left her desk for a moment and came back to an empty lobby. You had snuck down the hallway and knocked on the head honcho's door. His name was Toby. You introduced yourself, and said you needed a job. You told him if he hired you, you would name your firstborn child after him. He liked your tenacity.

When you knocked on that door, you opened a world of opportunity for our family. You not only chose my brother-to-be's name, you also put into motion years of adventures, stories and good times.

Dad, you were passionate about living the good life, craved adventure and excitement. While so many were busy keeping up with the Joneses, you planned our family's next adventure. We spent months out of school living in huts on beaches in Thailand, riding mopeds in Greece, waking up to Christmas in Hawaii, climbing in Kenya, and driving through France.

You did things that embarrassed me. Now, I find much joy in

the memories. You tightly held my hand in an elevator while you sang an African war chant for everyone to hear. You knocked on doors in France, asking strangers if we could pitch a tent in their fields, creating lifelong friendships in the process. In many ways, you turned water to wine. You created opportunities and friends, and rejoiced in others' stories, successes, and precious moments. You manifested your dreams through sheer grit and determination. Although you would likely have quickly dismissed manifesting talk, you were a master at creating what you wanted.

Your mottos were:

"Buy, buy, buy! Never sell, never sell, never sell!" This saying was in regard to real estate. Although you did sell, and then lamented about it for years, much to Mom's chagrin.

"Cash is king!" was another favorite.

"Education is key, education is key, education is key." You had a way of repeating things to bring them home.

The all-time family favorite was: "Keep it cheap and simple." (We actually had a T-shirt made up for that one.) In truth, you weren't cheap, you were generous. You took care of those in need, shared windfalls with the family, and opened your doors to acquaintances and strangers needing a meal and a warm bed.

You laughed hard at your mistakes. Like the time you put the roof of the shed on upside down. Or when you showered at the villagers' common water station in Nepal. Getting rid of the dirt and the grime from your journey while villagers pointed, laughed and stared, then slowly became hysterical with laughter as a llama peed directly from the ledge above the waterspout onto you. You did not laugh in that moment, you were horrified. But you taught us to look back at life and take humor from mistakes, hardship, and life's twists and turns.

Most times when I think of you, there is a touch of pain with the memory. A loss I still feel. Not just for losing you, but also for my lack of understanding of who you were, until it was too late.

Dad, the loss I felt when you passed was like nothing I'd ever experienced. It was as if I'd been hit by something large, that hit leaving a gaping hole. Near the end, everyone but me knew you were dying. I suppose deep down somewhere, I must have known too. But far deeper than that was the belief that you could never die. You were too strong in life, too big a character. Your stories and laughter boomed in rooms. When you passed away, the hole you left. . .well, let's just say, I realized that you had filled much of the space that shaped and defined me.

Of course, people said that losing you would get easier with time. Many years later, my grief has softened. In some ways, losing you has been a painful gift. Like a sapling under a mighty oak, shaded and unable to receive enough light to fully grow, your passing helped me to allow in more light, and to grow faster and stronger.

Near the end, by the river when you were still well enough go for a walk in the sun, you apologized to me for your extreme parenting. It was an apology I would not accept. I told you there was no need to apologize, that I loved everything about my childhood, and wouldn't change a thing. Dad, if you can read this tribute to you, I get it. I accept your apology, and I still wouldn't change a thing.

You were passionate in living a good life, a life full of adventure and excitement, and you took all of us with you. You wanted the best for us. You led us up mountains, through valleys, onto beaches, into deserts, onto islands, and to countries all over the world. You showed us all this life has to offer. You told us to go for it and gave us a head start. You wanted us to take advantage of all of the privileges you worked so hard to achieve.

Perhaps one of the biggest gifts you gave us was marrying a woman who loved you for all your idiosyncrasies, character and extremes. A woman who moved as one with you, supporting you, loving you, adventuring with you. In return, you loved her hard, took care of her, and made her feel special every day. A shining example of what it is to be a supportive partner, she was your secret weapon, and you knew it. Brilliant and beautiful, Mom demonstrated that a woman could be adventurous and feminine. She rocked hiking boots and high heels, and Dad, she still does.

At your celebration of life, your loss filled the room. Many joked that if you'd been there, you would have had everyone busy rock picking the nearby field. No matter who visited us on the farm, whether they were eighty-five years old or five years old, they picked a few rocks. You loved that. Everybody loved that.

As we grieved you, person after person approached me with praise for you.

"Your dad co-signed my first mortgage when no one else would."

"Your dad helped me with my first business."

"Your dad was a great man."

"Your dad is the reason I live in the Yukon."

"Your dad changed my life."

The list of genuine and much-deserved praise for you went on and on.

Endless praise.

Relentless praise.

I was so hard on you, Dad. I thought you were so hard on me. When I was a teenager, you used to laugh before saying, "One day, you will have teens of your own and you'll understand."

Well, Dad, I get it. You have probably been laughing pretty hard for a few years now.

With two teens in the house and a husband who works hard like you did, more than anything, I wish I could go back in time. If I could, I would give myself a little more understanding and openness so that I could fully appreciate you when you were alive.

You, the mighty oak, always let in enough light for this sapling to grow. The sheer immensity of your size and strength weathered me from many storms and mighty winds, allowing me to grow deep roots, my trunk strong, my branches reaching towards the sun.

As this realization hit, another truth immediately followed. The ironic, mind-bending epiphany that this acorn didn't fall far from the tree.

About Jennie Potter

Jennie Potter lives in a small town on Vancouver Island with her husband, Dave, and her two step-kids. Jennie is an inspirational speaker and coach who helps people add fuel to their passions, earn an income from home, and live their best lives. Leading by example, as a network marketing coach, she continually builds her own business to demonstrate the skills needed to succeed in the industry.

Jennie is currently working on her first book. In her free time, she loves writing, traveling, hiking and taking long baths. Her favorite scripture is from Mathew 5:14 (MSG): "You're here to be light, bringing out the God-colors in the world."

Connect with Jennie Potter
E-Mail: jennie.potter@hotmail.com
Facebook: https://www.facebook.com/mrsjenniepotter

Journey #7

LISTEN TO THE WHISPERS

Jennifer Marie Luce

The title of this chapter, "Listen to the Whispers," references my ever-expanding spiritual journey as I recalculated around a variety of happenings, including my attempted suicide, ovarian cancer, and romantic relationships. As it helped me greatly, throughout my story, I share what I've come to know about the ancient Chinese practice of medical qigong.

Qigong is a spiritually-based, mind-body practice that improves one's mental and physical health through postures, movement, breathing techniques and focused intention. Through exercises and guided meditations, a medical qigong practitioner manipulates qi energy to restore health and wellness. Continued well-being is maintained through individual meditative practices.

"Qi" (pronounced "chee") refers to the vital energy that flows through all things in the universe and acts as the bridge between matter and spirit. "Gong" (pronounced "gung") refers to achievement through practice or self-discipline. The ancient Chinese mastered specific techniques to balance the body's energy (qi) in order to live in harmony with the ever-changing environment (earth qi) and the universal (heaven qi) energetic field.

Qi as an energy can manifest within the body through three primary levels: 1) physically as matter (essence, marrow, blood and body fluids); 2) energetically as resonant vibrations (heat, sound, light, and electromagnetic fields); and 3) spiritually as divine light (beliefs, thoughts and feelings).

I hope you enjoy and benefit from reading about my journey

Jennifer Marie

* * *

The television commercial for the 2017 Jeep Compass was brilliant. In the commercial, you hear the electronic female voice of a virtual assistant say, “In fifteen meters, turn left.”

A man looks left and continues straight.

The virtual assistant says, “Recalculating.”

“Go straight to a steady job.”

A woman looks at her workplace, then turns around and heads in another direction.

“Recalculating.”

“Stay single until you’re thirty-four.”

A man proposes.

“Recalculating.”

You get the point. The words of the virtual assistant in the commercial represents societal expectations. The actors ignore what’s expected and follow their hearts. The premise of the message is that Chrysler (the company that sells the Jeep brand) wants to help you find your true north via the Jeep Compass.

In truth, finding one’s true north requires much more than a vehicle or compass.

Whispers of Trauma – Recalculating

At an August 2018 medical qigong and acupuncture appointment, my doctor of traditional Chinese medicine observed that there was an interesting juxtaposition between the intensely beautiful, loving and nurturing support of my amazing mother during my gestation—and the trauma of my birth.

The umbilical cord wrapped around my neck, I exited the womb in distress and abruptly entered the world via a caesarean section. My mother lost a lot of blood. We both almost died. Likely not wanting to continue with the agreement to do all the work I was sent here to do, my soul attempted to pull the plug on my life. The awareness of just how tough life could be must have settled into me during those moments.

Forty-one years later, I recognize that my precarious entrance into the world has allowed me to journey through the darkness of despair and return to the lightness of love, and to understand that for light to exist there must be dark. As a child, I was terrified of making even the simplest decision. After that medical qigong and acupuncture appointment, and a few other revelations that I share in this chapter, I now make decisions without fear. I trust that regardless of what path I choose, I will always be supported, my internal compass recalculating until I am steered in the right direction. Although it might take a bit longer than the universe intended, I find comfort in knowing that I am always loved, always moving in the right direction.

Whispers of Hopelessness – Recalculating

Following my parents' divorce and then the death of my mother's second husband, I spiraled into a deep depression. When my boyfriend of three years ended our relationship, I free-fell to my emotional bottom. Unable to focus, I quit college and turned to partying to fill the dark emptiness that haunted me twenty-four seven. I smoked and drank excessively. When that didn't sufficiently numb my pain, I cut myself. I chose men based on my feelings of deservedness—ones who treated me like dirt. The more a man yelled, hit and took advantage of me, the more needed and wanted I felt. Suicide was constantly on my mind. When it felt like killing myself slowly was taking too long, I took matters into my own hands. One by one, I swallowed pills and chased each down with booze.

Mom took me to Europe to help me heal. When we returned to Canada, I broke up with my boyfriend and enrolled in eighteen-month-long, twice-weekly psychodynamic support group at the local hospital in Richmond, British Columbia, where I lived. The group was led by Dr. Dahi, a psychiatrist. He often spoke about the fun in being free. "Just imagine what it would feel like to have fun in your experiences. These hard things you're holding onto can be let go. They can be awakened and released." The first time I heard him say this, I thought he was a quack. I hurt all the time and often felt like I was dying. *How the hell was I going to find any fun in my experiences?*

Over time, I began to trust him and his process. The eight members created connections that we explored within the safety of the group. We weren't permitted to communicate with one another outside of the group. I went through the process completely sober. No pharmaceuticals, no alcohol, no marijuana. I committed to healing myself.

I sobbed in this group.

People yelled and screamed, sometimes at each other.

Every form of conflict you can imagine came up in that group.

I learned how to talk about everything I was feeling.

I learned how to cry in front of people and be okay with it, something I'd been terrified of in the past (so much expression repression).

I learned how to sing and dance in my car and not care about what anybody else thought. I learned to stop hiding and not to seek answers outside of myself. I am grateful for Dr. Dahi's guidance and wisdom. His work in that group is a model that should be passionately grasped and inserted ferociously into parenting books and educational systems.

Most people have never been taught how to express themselves in healthy ways, making life particularly difficult for anyone who was neglected, abandoned or abused as a child. Before Dr. Dahi's group, I was often stumped regarding what I was feeling. Studying Dr. Robert Plutchik "Wheel of Emotions" on the Internet helped me further understand the gamut of emotions people experience.

For most of us, unhealed emotions from childhood are retriggered in our adult relationships. For some, retriggering brings them to a boiling point, a point where their anger or hurt is so intense it's painful. Left unhealed, these burn-marks can cause a person to react intensely. Once one learns how to recognize, work through, and heal their burn-marks, residual emotions from childhood lose their potency. There forward, the person can choose how to respond or react in emotionally-charged interactions and situations, and move onto a healthier, almost opposite experience.

Many years later, I spoke to someone at work about my journey in Dr. Dahi's group. "I dove deep down into the mucky waters of an abyss and played around in it. I got to see what all the fuss was about. 'Oh, here you are,' I said to the darkness. 'I'm just going to stomp and splash around in you. Get myself *really* dirty and see what you're all about.'"

My co-worker smiled.

"Well, it seems you're on the mend," he said.

I confidently exclaimed, "Oh, no. I'm good. I'm so good now. I'm mended. I faced many of the scary demons and walked right through that damn fire! Really wasn't that scary once the light got shone on it all."

I think I was a bit too expressive, as he gave me a shy grin before we both walked off in separate directions.

I love exploring such topics with people. Not out of pride or ego, but out of the hope it will inspire others to have the courage to broach the areas of their lives that scare or trouble them. Without a doubt, our medical system would be far less taxed if we all learned to express ourselves compassionately and constructively. Without the need to act out repressed childhood anger, there might even be fewer wars.

Whispers of Disease – Recalculating

Many cancers show subtle signs of existence. Often, when major symptoms arise the cancer has progressed. Listening to the whispers of our *feelings* is important to our overall health because we can learn from and heal or reverse the effects of trauma and unexpressed emotion that manifests in our bodies as disease.

In 2006, a few years into a romantic relationship, I was diagnosed with a rare form of ovarian cancer. My exciting life came to a screeching halt. Afraid of losing me, my boyfriend started to withdraw. Having lost my nana to breast cancer a few years prior, I equated my diagnosis with death. It didn't matter that I had an insanely high percentage of being cured, my heart couldn't hear that. I was petrified. My world crumbled again. *Why when things were going fairly good did something always have to happen?*

Chemotherapy caused most of my hair to fall out. To show her support, when I went to have my head shaved, my best friend sat in the next chair and had her head shaved too. Though it helped that we were both bald, much of my identity centered on my once long, blond hair. I couldn't look at my steroid-puffy face and baldheaded-self in the mirror and see the old me anymore, whoever that was.

Throughout my treatments, I fought to maintain my sense of dignity and independence. It was a battle I lost. After being on my own for six years, at age twenty-nine, at her insistence, my Mom moved in with me during my treatments. Having to let go of my pride and be vulnerable was truly tough for me. However, without Mom's loving care and patience, I can only imagine what might have happened to me. She drove me to appointments, cooked my meals, and encouraged me to eat even though nothing would stay down. I was grateful for all that she did, including how gracefully she handled my over-emotional chemo-induced-menopausal moodiness. She truly loved me for me.

My boyfriend did his best to make me feel loved and hopeful. Though I didn't believe him, it helped that he continued to call me Beautiful. Barely able to cope with my own feelings, I did little to help him process his. Several months after the completion of twenty horrific chemotherapy treatments, we broke up. I was devastated. I'd thought he was my soul mate.

Along with him went our plans for the future. Everything else I had planned, no longer felt right. Getting a puppy, Lucy, was my saving grace. When I couldn't even look at myself in the mirror, she showed me unconditional love. Cute with a personality to match, she harnessed everyone's attention, taking the focus off of me.

By the end of the chemo treatments, fibromyalgia had settled into every joint in my body and I walked like an old arthritic woman. Also suffering from chemo-induced memory loss, I had to retrain my brain. I couldn't remember simple words such as pen, chair, and table, which made me feel stupid. Each time this happened, I thought, "My vocabulary was once fairly extensive, what happened?" Afraid that the overwhelming workload and stress of my job had caused or contributed to my cancer, I dreaded returning to work.

I realized that the universe had knocked me off my feet to get my attention. For me, cancer's message was, "Okay, Jen. It's time to wake up, sweetheart. You recognize that you're not doing what you're meant to do." The trouble was that I had no idea what I was meant to do.

After a year-and-a-half of convalescing, feeling beholden to them for paying my way while I got well, I returned to my old job. Forcing myself to stay focused on my desire for a better life, I quickly fell back into my "old normal" work and life routines.

Initially, I didn't grasp that having survived cancer I was a different person. I kept working hard but developed an overwhelming desire to give back to the world for allowing me to live. I volunteered to support young adult cancer survivors thinking it would help me heal as well. I felt accepted and appreciated, however, the loss of many people that I was trying to support, took its toll on my health and frame of mind.

I tried my hardest to be the person I had been before: perfect at most things, dedicated, hardworking, a multitasker and an overachiever. I strove for new, more challenging positions, but wasn't getting interviewed. My health still wasn't the best, I took sick leave too often, and my employer didn't consider me "reliable" enough to be entrusted with a new position. After years of persistence, I was finally offered an incredible opportunity helping to lead a high-profile project. It was the chance to shine and get the recognition and appreciation that I had been waiting for. At long last, I had proven myself worthy of something great that would be my own. Someone believed in me.

Having taken the advice of my numerologist, Joseph Ghabi, I had begun using my full name Jennifer Marie. It was hard to get accustomed to it, but the more I used it, the more confident I felt. Without a doubt, the new name vibration gifted me with a degree of personal power that eventually led to my being offered the position.

It soon became clear that the project was more than I could handle. The expectations were too great, the hours too long, and the workload too heavy. The new me couldn't manage all that anymore; nor did the new me want to manage all that anymore. I asked for assistance from my superiors. It was to no avail. They basically told me that I had to do whatever the project demanded of me. I felt responsible and couldn't walk away from the job.

Words that Joseph had said to me at the numerology course kept repeating in my head, "It's time to stop playing small. People are waiting to hear what you have to say. Do you want to keep them waiting?"

I didn't *want* to keep people waiting, I wanted to build my career *and* touch lots of people through writing, teaching and speaking. The only problem was I didn't have the time, energy or any clue of what path to take.

I heard the universe again yelling at me, "Okay, Jennifer Marie. We aren't joking anymore! You're not listening hard enough. Do what you are meant to do!" I ran to Joseph for spiritual advice, but I still wasn't hearing what he had to say.

Every day my chest felt so tight from anxiety that I thought I was having mini heart attacks. My body was in constant physical pain from sitting at a desk, sometimes for over twelve hours. I was hypervigilant and jumped at every unexpected sound or movement. Evenings and weekends, I tried to catch up by working from home. I couldn't concentrate when awake and couldn't sleep when I went to bed. Tired and overwhelmed, I didn't have the energy or desire to eat healthy food. Burned out and afraid I was headed for another major health collapse, I had no choice but to go on sick leave.

I felt like a complete failure. I'd let myself and the team down. Unworthiness and shame drifted back into my life like a heavy fog. I didn't deserve *any* of the wonderful things life had to offer—love, abundance or happiness. It took a conversation with my mom for me to fully appreciate an inner-knowing I'd recently identified.

"Honey, what do you mean you don't feel worthy? I don't understand."

"Mom, I am not saying that I am less worthy than anyone else. The problem is that I don't feel worthy. There's something amiss inside of me and I cannot love myself completely and unconditionally."

"I still don't understand," Mom said, sounding loving and genuinely concerned.

"What I'm saying is that I've been fighting for love, acceptance and acknowledgement outside of myself. What I didn't realize until recently is that I first need to foster, experience and celebrate those qualities within myself."

After we hung up, it struck me that it hadn't been enough to *use* my full name, I needed to *live* my full name. To do this, I had to finish clearing past hurts and more deeply connect with my spiritual-self so that I could identify and live my divine purpose.

Trusting the universe, I began listening to my intuition and paying attention to the lessons behind the people I met and the opportunities being presented. I heard them as possible ways to free myself from past cycles. When introduced to people who could make my dream of becoming a published author a reality, I heard them and acted.

I read books by and listened to famous gurus such as Napoleon Hill, Bob Proctor, Mike Dooley, Lola Jones, Beautiful Chorus, and Wayne Dyer. Recognizing that they were powerful manifestors, I paid closer attention to my thoughts and spoken words. What I believed and expressed would be what I received.

Still recovering from the major fatigue associated with burnout, coupled with dealing with ongoing anxiety, depression and unexplainable physical pain, created an upward battle and conflict with the new perspectives I was learning and incorporating into my life. For the first time, I felt that I was worth the effort it took to transition through this uncomfortableness. For once, I welcomed changes in my life. I wanted to change.

Whispers of Change – Recalculating

My numerologist, Joseph Ghabi, had become a mentor of mine. Joseph encouraged me to "cut" the darkest deepest crap I'd been holding on to. During one of our conversations about the process of consciously and properly letting go, he said, "There's another side to you. A higher version of yourself that is deeply connected with all that is good and amazing. Find out what he or she looks like, feels like, smells like. What she or he feels like in all her or his beautiful strong, joyous energy that is connected with all magnificent abundance. What is a day like in her or his shoes?"

It took me a long time to have any comprehension of what

Joseph was talking about. It took me longer to see *her* vibrancy and power, to imagine and meditate on *her* gloriousness.

I was so lost.

I had given myself away to those around me. I focused on the external as I tried to make others happy. To be honest, I was stuck.

Then, along came Mel.

I met Mel at one of Joseph's numerology events: Consciously Living Your Destiny. At the time, I was living in Richmond, a small city on the outskirts of Vancouver, British Columbia. On an island, most of the land is less than three feet above sea level. Numerous dykes keep the muddy, clay-like alluvial soil from flooding.

The girlfriend I attended Joseph's event with was immediately smitten with Mel. I was intrigued that a handsome, intelligent, young man was interested in learning about himself. Noting that her attraction to Mel was strong, I didn't pursue him romance-wise.

When my relationship with this girlfriend began to wane, I started spending more time with a coworker. When Mel and my now estranged girlfriend stopped dating, he rented a room in my coworker's place. I found it interesting that Mel's and my paths had again crossed. One night after an extremely overwhelming day, while visiting with my coworker at her place, I asked her to give Mel my phone number.

Coincidentally, a few days later when Mel and I went on our first date (watching the stars on a cloudless summer's eve), I received a note from my doctor to take a leave of absence from work. The stress of leading a high-profile work project had taken a toll on my health.

It was a paramount time.

A sweet, gentle spirit, Mel listened to me with his heart and ears. When he suggested moving to Vancouver, I paid attention. I'd lived in Richmond for thirty-two years and had finally figured out how stuck in the boggy mud of the city I'd been. Although it is a lovely place, it didn't resonate with me.

Vancouver is a beautiful coastal metropolis backdropped by mountains. Thanks to hosting Expo in 1986 and the Olympic Games in 2010, this world-class city is known globally. I am one of the rare few to be born and raised in Vancouver. I often joke that I should be on display in a museum.

Over the years, the sense of the city has changed. A favorite destination for travelers and explorers, it's become quite transient. It's emotionally "colder" than it used to be, however, it has a substantial population of awakened and holistic-minded individuals. Moving to Vancouver played a significant role in my ability to grow and awaken further.

When he recognized what I was doing, Mel encouraged me to lose the *control* I thought I needed to cope with all the trauma my sensitive body, mind and spirit had been holding. Stifling my *emotions*, *needs* and *wants* was a coping strategy I'd deliberately mastered, not at all understanding how harmful it was to my well-being.

As it was with my meeting Mel, people tend to attract those we need to teach us lessons and help us get over and through the biggest burn-marks in our lives. I think we also attract people who inspire growth experiences. Understandably, if someone isn't normalized toward healthy and socially-appropriate behaviors, these lessons can be unsettling, even frightening.

Over time, in an in-your-face loving way, Mel taught me how to let go of the sense of control I thought I needed to deal with trauma. Trauma that resonated not just from physical happenings such as my difficult birth, car accidents, and cancer, but also trauma from repressed emotions and emotions embedded in my DNA from past generations. Reading *It Didn't Start With You: How Inherited Family Trauma Shapes Who We Are and How to End the Cycle* by Mark Wollyn helped me to fully understand epigenetics and to release negative emotions rooted deep within the cells of my body.

Whispers of Pain – Recalculating

When I moved to Vancouver in the fall of 2015, I became acutely aware of the smell of nearby trees and a sporadic stabbing pain around my left shoulder blade. Whenever I walked in Pacific Spirit Park during times when I was negating my meditative practices or giving credence to negative thoughts, my shoulder pain would present. It wasn't until an enlightening medical qigong session in June 2018 that I realized the cause of the pain.

Having read *Eastern Body, Western Mind* by Anodea Judith, I knew that the left side of the body is considered feminine, and the right side, masculine. I suspected that the sporadic stabbing pain in my left shoulder was somehow related to my maternal connection with my mom's deceased mother.

Countless times after her death in 2003, Nana showed herself in my dreams. She's my parking genie and somehow plucked me out and kept me safe in several car accidents. I've connected with Nana's younger-self through meditation.

When she was dying in the hospital, Nana acted as if she were possessed by demons. She spoke in tongue and hissed when shown the cross. Having denied Nana last rites, when Mom persisted that her mother "wasn't there," the priest cried and shook his head.

At Nana's request, my brother and I weren't allowed to visit her. In response to my wanting closure with Nana before she left her earthly form, Mom said, "She doesn't want you to remember her like this." I wrote Nana a letter to say goodbye. During our final telephone conversation, I was grateful when she acknowledged receiving and reading it.

I found it odd that although she didn't want my brother and I to see her before she died, the casket was open during Nana's service. I will never forget her twisted and tormented expression. The grief, the anger, the resentment she held, it all showed on her face.

During my June 2018 medical qigong session, I learned that a divine light energy does not present as pain. When I chose to acknowledge this and thanked the entity for showing me to *reconnect* to and *practice* in nature, it disappeared. It let go. I felt it leave my back as a cold, slimy, black, worm-like essence.

Soon after, acutely aware that my divined path included a deep connection with the earth and spiritually-based practices such as meditation, I created my "Mother Nature's Garden" business. I learned how to dry herbs and blend teas; how to make flower essences, lavender wands, and health and beauty serums and tonics; how to create jewelry from mother earth's stones and crystals; and how to concoct moon and gemstone elixirs. A Tera Mai Seichem Reiki Master, in addition to products, I also offer energy healing.

Whispers of Growth – Recalculating

When we first began dating, Mel asked me three successive questions: "Do you understand what grounding is? Do you know how to ground yourself? Are you grounded?" At the time, I thought I was grounded so answered a resounding yes to all three questions. Many years later, I experienced a new truth.

This new truth happened shortly after a medical qigong session. Toward the end of the session, the practitioner said, "Bring in the light from above through your crown and into your heart. Your heart wishes to speak and open."

"Yes," I thought to myself, "this is a repeat of what I'm learning through my oracle card readings and what my intuition has been feeling."

"Once you bring that energy into your heart, radiate it out through you...all your energy centers won't only balance, but you will manifest and walk more truly in your purpose...operate *from* and *in* love."

A few days later, I was practicing my connection with the earth in the park across the street from my Vancouver apartment. There was a piece of malachite on my right knee, Botswana agate on my left, and adorned in jewelry made of ruby, pink tourmaline, cobaltite calcite and Peruvian pink opal. Eyes closed, my back resting against the curved trunk of a Hemlock tree, I focused on my heart and breathed deeply, easily and fully feeling my connection with Mother earth.

The contrast was remarkable. When Mel had asked his three successive questions, I'd been living in Richmond for decades. It's energy distracting, the city's muddy, clay-like alluvial soil likely played a role in my inability to fully ground. Vancouver's earth is much more stable and has an inviting spiritual energy. When I lived in Richmond, although I thought I did, I didn't have a clue about what it was to be grounded in all the ethereal bodies of the physical, mind/emotion and spirit. In Vancouver, I felt spiritually grounded to Mother Earth and enjoyed the sense of freedom that emanates from her and the divine above.

Whispers of Love - Recalculating

My romantic relationship before Mel had felt like a cage with too many rules, and ultimately, an unavailable partner. For me, Mel represented the opposite.

My twin-flame relationship with Mel was a big one. It was tumultuous. And tough. And beautiful. And encompassed the biggest relationship lessons I may ever learn. It was an opportunity I wasn't aware I needed. We were two people on similar paths of self-growth and understanding, and what I discovered was that I was so ready for the big one. The One. All of it.

Intuitively sensing that it was the truth, when we started dating, I told Mel that we were just each other's teachers, that we wouldn't stay physically together for life. Ours was a challenging, in-your-face relationship filled with unconditional kindness, real love and an understanding of the many lessons it and we had to offer. Together, we explored and expanded our understanding of acceptance, compassion, patience, boundaries, and so much more.

Our physical journey as a couple concluded by mutual agreement. I still had lessons of my own that needed to be ironed out. Mel did as well. Our respective lessons needed to be experienced without each other.

My experiences *with Mel* and *through him* took me to a new place of release, deeper acceptance and opening. When our relationship ended, I realized that it was going to take time to fully understand its breadth.

A pattern of mine had been attaching to unavailable men whose focus was seemingly on something more important than me. To protect myself, I closed off my heart in hopes of avoiding heartbreak at the end of a future romantic relationship. Part of my solo journey forward after separating from Mel included focusing on healing and reopening my heart.

A former spiritual teacher of mine, Lola Jones, mentioned that many etheric/light individuals regard relationships differently, not focusing or holding expectations around "forever." Lola advises that having someone in your life is often for a reason, a season or a lifetime, and that it is wise to be grateful for the experience, thankful for the lessons, and to let go when it ends.

I was raised around the premise that the vows of marriage somehow miraculously guide us and hold us in the space of "till death do us part." Maybe this premise wasn't meant to be taken so seriously. I believe we are connected with each other until we die regardless of whether we are physically together. If the other has an unhealthy hold on us, then energetic cord-cutting may be necessary to release the negative energy so that one can grow and move forward unhindered.

Memories of another will never be lost. Our relationship experiences help to shape us and assist each of us in further understanding our true self. I have gratitude and love for all the life experiences that I've made happen or have invited into my life.

When I look back at the last fifteen years, I see all the weavings of life's magic. I am grateful for this wonderous web of lessons that gets stuck in places I've forgotten, ready to have light shone on it and released.

Whispers of Purpose – Recalculating

The ending to the Jeep Compass commercial is: "Love, hope,

happiness. Whatever your destination, there's a million beautiful, ever-changing ways to get there." I couldn't agree more. Life has a way of changing things around to steer each of us toward our universe-intended path—our purpose.

As a Gemini snake, I've discovered an ongoing path to oneness-in-self by listening to what's around me and connecting with Mother Earth, Father Sky, Grandmother Moon, and Grandfather Sun. Heeding the silenced whispers of pain in my left shoulder blade, I listen to the continued energetic whispers of nature. I strive to hear the wisdom of my ancestors and truly listen. I do my best to distinguish between what's mine and what belongs to those around me. I seek the connections between what I feel in the physical and emotional/mental realms and how they interconnect.

The practice of qigong has changed my life for the best. I learned how to ground with the energy of the earth, to connect with the divine energy of the universe, and let go of energy that isn't mine or in some way holds me back. Through my qigong meditative practices, I continue to learn: to harbor acceptance, kindness and compassion for myself first, then others; to create gratitude for all that is; and to *not* settle and stay in the dark, conditioned, negative energies focused on lack. Although I'm still learning, I'm able to focus on the energy of abundance more fully.

I feel that I'm on the precipice of something great. Without measuring it or putting it in a box, there's something exciting about being free. I'm aware that it will be a lifelong journey into self as I continually awaken to a higher version of me.

"And the day came when the risk to remain tight in a bud was more painful than the risk it took to blossom."
— Anais Nin

About Jennifer Marie Luce

Jennifer Marie Luce lives in Vancouver, British Columbia. She is a writer, poet, artist, dancer, singer, intuitive, energy healer, lover of the creative, and a daughter of Mother Nature.

Jennifer Marie's love of travel has taken her to seventeen countries and more than a hundred cities. She enjoys digging in deeply to assist others in healing themselves and identifying their paths.

Jennifer Marie is available to speak to audiences about a number of healing modalities and life challenges.

Connect with Jennifer Marie Luce
E-Mail: turnurlifearound@gmail.com

Journey #8

WELCOME HOME!

Josephine Lavallee

Do I stay or do I go? My gap year after high school began with a life-altering question followed by a series of what ifs. There was no right or wrong answer, only choices. I had brain fog.

Doing what teenage girls do to attract boyfriends, three girlfriends and I swam at the beach in our itty bitty bikinis. Equipped with baby oil, an oversized beach towel, a romance novel, and a transistor radio, I settled into the sandy spot we had claimed to bake in the sun. The darker the tan the better it looked.

I appeared younger than my girlfriends, perhaps because I was small for my age and had an athletic body shape. Like bees to honey, I had no problem attracting a boy's attention. In 1964, long, sexy, glamorous, soft, smooth and silky hair was a fashion statement. I could only dream of it. I felt beautiful with my fine, ash-blonde hair styled short above my shoulders in a bob. Not one to follow fashion, I think, as a result, I began to hatch an independent personality.

A major decision I'd made would affect my life's path and my destiny. *Who am I? Was I reluctantly heading in the wrong direction?* I wanted to know.

I was eighteen. With my high school graduation completed, saying good-bye to all things familiar, I was flying overseas in September for twelve months to become more fluent in French and

German. At the same time, I would be studying some academic British A-Level subjects which would equate to a North American grade thirteen diploma. Being the first person in my family to reach for the stars, my heart's desire was to attend the University of Victoria with my girlfriends from high school. Unfortunately, I had not accumulated enough credits to reach my goal. The British A-Level diploma would provide me with enough credits to enroll in our local university.

Raised to be stay-at-home moms, in Canada at that time, girls were not given the same opportunities as boys. Girls were raised foremost to be good mothers, volunteer in their community and support their husbands. First comes love, then comes marriage, then comes mommy pushing the baby carriage. My parents were born at the turn of the century and adopted ideas inherited through their ancestral lineage. My parents believed that to be successful, my sister and I should marry well. In their eyes, what I needed was a good man to take care of me. My parents viewed my year studying abroad as a way to improve my marketability as a wife.

In stark contrast, 1964 was the beginning of the revolutionary sixties. We baby boomers sought careers before considering motherhood. Several of my friends never wanted to get married. I craved independence, not dependence. A free thinker, I wasn't interested in fulfilling someone else's dreams.

The little girl within me, unsure of who she was and too shy to argue, felt conflicted. I trusted my parents knew what was best for me. I desperately wanted their approval and to follow a life path they'd clearly defined for me. No one in our family had attended university. *Did it make it a wrong decision for my life path?*

A hormonal teenager, growing up, my mood swings

fluctuated between excitement and sadness. I struggled with self-worth, sometimes questioning if I knew truly what was best for my future.

On a bright August afternoon, Mother and I were upstairs in the spare bedroom strategizing what to pack in my blue and gold steamer trunk, and alternatively, what to pack in my flight luggage. On the school's suggested list were pajamas, pillowcases and twin-size sheet sets, hiking boots, coat, knitted toque, slippers, toiletries, books, pens, spiral-ring notepaper, and French and German dictionaries. Items we decide to add were all things winter, including heavy wool socks, ski anorak, ski boots, snowsuit and mittens.

The headmistress preferred to be addressed as *Principal*. According to her instructions, it was cheapest to ship the heavier items in advance via the Panama Canal, across the Atlantic Ocean to France, and then by railcar to Switzerland. Giving my steamer trunk an eight week head start, the plan was to have my trunk arrive at Tah Dorf International School before me.

Two years older than me, my boyfriend was my high school sweetheart. Born in London, Ontario, he was an officer cadet at the Royal Military College near where I lived in Victoria. Although I'd casually dated an airline pilot, a grocery store clerk, and a lacrosse player, the army lieutenant was my preferred dance partner. Before I left for Europe, I wanted to spend as much time as possible with him.

One August evening, the music throbbed to the band's drumming. My boyfriend and I and two other couples who were his friends sat around a table, drinking, munching on crunchy snacks and talking. From comments he had made, I knew this officer cadet truly loved me, cherished me for my uniqueness, for placing other people's needs before my own, for my genuine interest in individuals from other nations, and for my daringness to dance uninhibited. After all, it was the sixties.

I embraced him warmly as we moved rhythmically to the music. Atop navy dress pants, he wore his Royal Military College formal, scarlet, dress uniform fastened at the neck with gold epaulets and gold buttons. His black shoes were polished so brightly they reflected the light. I was impressed. While we were on the dance floor, a number of sub-lieutenants acknowledged him with a nod. In the mess hall, he saluted his senior officers or avoided them entirely. His age and sophistication made my local boyfriends seem somewhat less mature and less attractive.

When not on duty, writing college examines, or on parade, he practically lived at my parents' house. During scheduled leave from duty at work, he would arrange for a taxi to pick us up, and we'd go out for dinner. Sometimes, he'd have dinner with my family. On weekends, we'd take long afternoon walks, go sailing, listen to live music at the Cellar coffee house, or share a bucket of buttery popcorn at a movie theater. When I expressed my fears and joys, he stood by me, empathizing with my deepest angst and tolerating my crazy mood swings of love and sorrow.

A week before I left, after a swanky party on the mezzanine floor of the Crystal Pool, my boyfriend and I drove home in a rented, burgundy Mustang convertible. It was two a.m., and I felt sleepy drunk from having had a good time dancing the night away. Under the porch light at the front door to my parents' house, he smiled and took both my arms in his. He leaned across to press his firm body next to mine. Then, he kissed me goodnight before saying, "I'll write you every day. And I promise I'll be here when you get back. I love you, Josée. I want to marry you."

Although I knew he was crazy about me, I hadn't anticipated

that he would propose. I was amazed. Never had I heard anything so astounding. He wanted to marry me!

"I promise I'll answer your letters," I said, unsure as to whether I wanted to be anyone's wife. My sister married at age twenty-one. Age eighteen, I knew I needed at least three or four more years to be single. *Would he wait for me?*

My passport told authorities who I was—a Canadian citizen with a one-year student visa to study in Europe. I changed flights in Toronto, Ontario, and bordered an Air Canada flight to Switzerland. When the plane landed in Zurich, it was early morning. The airport personnel spoke mostly in German. I showed my identification to an English speaking security person, and then followed the queue to the luggage pickup area. After collecting my luggage from the carousel, I made my way to the airport bus that would take me to the Swiss autobahn train station. Around hills, lakes and through long dusty tunnels, the express passenger train travelled alongside numerous alpine villages as it journeyed southward to my home away from home, Interlaken in the Bernese Alps.

From breathing dry dusty tunnel air, my throat wanted nourishment. I craved a lemon citron drink and perhaps a Swiss cheese sandwich on black pumpernickel bread. Whenever the train stopped, there were kiosks at the railway station. However, as the train was running on a precise time schedule, fearing that it might leave without me, I was too scared to jump off—jump on. I didn't disembark. Overtired and suffering from a lack of sleep during my flight, combined with jet lag, my thinking became hazy. I felt grouchy. Doubting myself, I didn't understand how capable an eighteen year old I truly was. I wondered: *What if nobody likes me? What if I don't pass my exams and the whole year is just frittered away, pointless?* In a drowsy state of consciousness, the train rocking back and forth lulled me to sleep, and I wearily closed my eyelids for about a half hour, shutting them softly. Being more of an optimist at heart, I directed my thoughts towards: *What if one year from now, all my hopes, dreams, ambitions and goals come true?* It excited me.

Shortly thereafter, I heard an electronic whistle announcing my destination. As the train slowed to a stop at the north autobahn station, I reached for my luggage, and stepped off the train onto the platform. I had arrived. This was Interlaken (meaning between two lakes).

The view took my breath away. Two lakes—aqua blue in color—a canal, green grass, a public park, and above all that, an enormous mountain covered in a glacial blanket of glistening snow. The majestic mountain, Jungfrau (meaning young lady), a picture-perfect display of nature's magnificence and strength dominated the scene. Renowned worldwide, international tourists travelled long distances to ski her icy slopes and courageously sweep down the Jungfrau's hairpin curves. I felt at home.

Leaving the busy main street behind me with its alpine shops and parklike setting, I hand gestured to an approaching taxi, and rode up the hill to the school. Without announcing that we'd arrived where I wanted to be, the taxi driver stopped the car, retrieved my bags from the trunk, and rudely grabbed my Swiss francs and left—giving me no change. Thankfully, the school's address was displayed on a decorative sign. Standing alone curbside, luggage beside me, I stared in awe at a dark brown chalet with a sloping roof, flower boxes and red shutters.

I waited a minute before knocking on the brown chalet door. Heidi, the woman I was told would greet me, opened the door and said, "Willkommen. Willkommen zu hause," as she motioned me inside with a wave of her hand.

On the floor were several pairs of shoes. I kicked off mine and followed Heidi into the common area where I was introduced to four British girls from South Africa. They appeared to be eighteen or nineteen years of age, physically fit, and seemed to be from a similar socioeconomic background as me, although I wasn't sure. They were all dressed in either a knee-length skirt and coordinating sweater or designer blue jeans with a white shirt.

I was immediately charmed by their appearances, vivid imaginations, spontaneous laughter and British accents. They introduced themselves using their nicknames: Huck, Flowers, Hen, and Mole. I later learned that Huck was short for Huckleberry friend from her favorite song *Moon River*; Flowers was for Rosemarie; Hen was for Henrietta; and Mole was for Maureen.

"My name is Josée," I said smiling nervously. The chatter that followed and their intense stares reminded me of what it was like to be a new girl at school. I was the only Canadian and the only student from North America. Josée was how they addressed me, but not for long. Within a few days, I earned the nickname Flickers, a bird from the woodpecker family that is native to North America.

I soon discovered that Welsh people had a reputation for their ability to sing like a bird. I think it might have something to do with the pronunciation of the Welsh Celtic language. My roommate, who was Welsh, often sang while in the shower, walking the staircase and when getting dressed. Day and night, her soprano voice reverberated throughout the chalet.

My first term, the fall semester, began two days after my arrival. Principal registered me in two French classes (one oral and one written) with Mademoiselle Danielle. My class in German was taught by Heidi.

My Dutch, Austrian and German classmates and the four girls from South Africa were proficient in either three or four languages. They spoke fluently in Dutch, German, French, English, and Afrikaans. During French and German oral classes, I was unable to keep up with them. Having a leg up on me, I felt like a fish out of water and lost. Without a clue what was going on linguistically, emotional crankiness dominated my behavior.

As the days passed, I started to feel like a numskull, and increasingly cut off and isolated from the others. Becoming more and more despondent with the lack of communication, I became homesick. *I wanted to leave.* My French and limited high school German were far below par at the international school. A quiet mouse, I listened intently, building my comprehension skills. But I was too shy to talk, felt self-conscious, and afraid to speak in case I embarrassed myself. To disguise my feeling of inadequacies, I decided to be obstinate and sometimes skipped class. Occasionally, when alone in my bedroom, soulful tears soaked my pillow. Sleeping in and not completing my homework became my new norm.

One day, Principal summoned me to her office. "Unsatisfactory. You know this, n'est-ce pas?" she said, annoyed. "Josée, if you wish to pass your A-level exams this semester, you'd better buckle up."

Feeling caught and verbally spanked, I knew that I couldn't slack off anymore. I had to put more effort into my studies. I cried at the end of the day. It was pitiful behavior even by my rebellious standards.

Each afternoon, between two and four o'clock, we had designated leisure time. We were free to simply sit outside in the sun socializing with fellow students, write oodles of letters home, or walk with friends into Interlaken for necessities, postage stamps, and a delicious ice coffee.

Keeping to his word, my boyfriend wrote me twice a week. Sending me ten page (or longer) handwritten letters, he'd sometimes tuck a trinket inside. With one letter, he included a magazine photo of a couple that he had cut into a heart shape. Another time, he sent a three-leaf clover that he'd obviously pressed between the pages of a book. They were tokens meant to show how much he missed me. Twice a month, he'd send a gigantic card with a funny saying or joke, and include a few of his own doodles. Once, he mailed a small parcel of Canadian memorabilia that included round lapel pins, pencils with a beaver decal, and other items he'd found at a tourist shop in Victoria. The accompanying letter said that he thought I'd enjoy exchanging the items with foreign students at school.

Even if I hadn't yet answered his previous letter, he'd airmail another. New mail was stacked on the chalet hall table. It usually arrived during our afternoon leisure time. When we returned from our walk into Interlaken, there'd often be a few letters for me, and my seemingly jealous roommates would tease me. Embarrassed, I'd blush. Aware that most of them seldom received mail from their boyfriends, I was never sure how to respond.

Late one night, all of us in our pajamas and in our rooms, someone called out, "I smell smoke."

"Fire!" bellowed another roomie.

Unnerved, excitement abounded. Six pairs of feet, one behind the other, thumped down the stairs. Switching on the lights, we spotted the wastebasket was on fire, inside and out. The flames, gray smoke and stinky smell startled us. Someone quickly doused the fire with water and took the charred basket outdoors.

Roe, our roomie from Jersey Island, one of the English Channel Islands, had thrown an ignited cigarette butt into the wastebasket before going to bed. It was November, and although smoking wasn't permitted in the chalet, Roe confessed that she'd smoked inside because of the bitterly cold north wind.

After a lively discussion about how lucky we were that Huckleberry had smelled smoke before we all fell asleep, and how we would have been trapped in our rooms with only a small upstairs window as a possible escape route, we all agreed not to tell Principal about the incident. With the sliding glass door open and the upstairs window ajar for ventilation, I went to bed wearing winter socks. Shivering under the duvet cover, deep sleep eluded me.

A few days later, with kindheartedness, we decided Roe should have a new nickname. As she was a good-natured Irish Catholic, we sprinkled her with water droplets as we christened her Sparky. As far I know, she never smoked in the house again.

Fortunately for me, the cigarette episode changed the ambiance in our chalet. Little by little, I discovered that school with dormitory roommates could be hilarious. Letting go of my more serious and uptight self, I was able to be silly once in a while, unlatching a playful side of me I hadn't known existed.

Our upcoming French A-level examination for the fall semester a week away, I was sitting on my bed studying when I heard a knock on my door. I called out, "It's open."

Huckleberry, a slim, pretty, South African girl about five-foot-two, with an angular chin and short dark hair, stepped into my room and sat at the foot of the bed. She radiated an impish smile. I knew instantly something was up.

"I'm wanting to play a practical joke on Sparky," she said. "What do you think? Let's do something to get back at her."

I knew she was referring to the burning cigarette in the wastebasket incident. Nodding, all smiles, and a twinkle in my eye, I said, "Let's apple pie her bed." I told Huckleberry the basic premise of the silly prank, and promised to demonstrate it the next time Sparky left the chalet.

A few days later, Sparky announced she wanted to go to town for the afternoon and asked if anyone wanted to go with her. Huckleberry and I exchanged glances. We shook our heads and claimed that we needed to study for the A-level French exam.

The coast clear, Huckleberry and I snuck into Sparky's room and stripped her bed. The bottom sheet with corners went into the laundry hamper, and the top sheet became the bottom sheet. After tucking the flat sheet around the top portion of the mattress, we folded the bottom half toward the top of the bed so that it appeared to be a top sheet. After smoothing out the wrinkles, we replaced the duvet and pillows. Our prize bed was designer ready. Giggling, we thought the prank was hysterical and couldn't wait to hear Sparky's reaction when she crawled into bed and couldn't stretch out her legs.

Huckleberry slept in a different room. That night when we went to bed, like me, I imagined that she was laying silently on her back listening for Sparky's auspicious response. We were not disappointed.

Sparky soon hollered, "Whoever did this, I'm going to get you."

I fell asleep smiling smugly.

As fall gave way to winter, needing a dose of nature's beauty, I watched from the sliding glass door as new falling snow accumulated in pillow-like pyramids on the black rod iron patio furniture. My first thought was, "If it's snowing here then it must be snowing on the mountain." My second thought was, "When do we go skiing?" I soon learned that ski school didn't start until January.

I flew to England for Christmas break. Following my holiday in Bournemouth and London, I returned to school feeling refreshed but nervous. No longer a new girl, I felt confident and comfortable about being there. What daunted me was that the second term was a full immersion program in German and French. During every activity—ski school, restaurant meals, shopping, nightclub disco dances, and movies—we weren't allowed to speak in English.

For the first few weeks, I struggled to communicate in small sentences. What a great relief I felt when we were in our bedrooms behind closed doors speaking in English where the real conversations happened.

I spoke to Principal before ski-school started, gently telling her that I had some experience skiing in Canada, owned a pair of ski boots and had skied both the beginner and intermediate ski trails on a mountain at home. She replied, "Nevertheless, I'm putting you in the beginners' class with the other students."

Feeling a little humiliated, I knew I couldn't win the argument, and reluctantly agreed to be in the baby class. In high school, sports of various kinds were what I excelled at. Flexible and agile, swimming, gymnastics, girl's field hockey, and skiing were favorite activities of mine.

On the bunny hill, the ski instructor showed us how to snowplow. Start pointing the tips of the skis together so you don't go too fast. Put your weight on your bent leg, the downhill leg and go one way. Then, shift your weight to the opposite leg and go the other direction. All day long, one behind the other, my classmates and I followed the ski instructor back and forth across the bunny slope, practicing our turns. At the end of the day, he let me know in German, that I'd done well, but I must slow down. "Verboten. Zu schnell," he said, telling me that I was going too fast.

After ski school on a weeknight, we often went for dinner at a busy restaurant frequented by locals. Not advertised on tourist brochures, the restaurant was hidden behind the main street of Interlaken. The restaurant exterior looked like a chalet. Inside, there were long wooden tables with benches that were made from planks. Each table having twelve place settings, we would sit six of us on one side and six of us on the opposite side. Although we later paid her back, Principal always ordered and paid for dinner: beef fondue for everyone.

Within a short while, two pots of cooking oil sat poised on Bunsen burners in the center of the table. Taking my turn cooking, I'd spike a slice of raw red meat onto the end of my long fondue fork, and dip it into the bubbling oil. When satisfied it was cooked, I then transferred the meat onto my plate and added mushrooms, red bell pepper strips, and thinly cut onion slices. A variety of sauces followed the meat into my mouth. Socializing with the class over a delicious meal unified us as a group. Although we always had fun, as we were the girls from the international school and easily recognized by the locals, we were expected to behave.

A few weeks into the second term, during one dinner, Principal shared her thoughts. She said that Henrietta and Cairo could advance to the next ski level. They looked delighted. My name went unannounced. *What!* Dumbfounded, in a subconscious reaction, I shook my head. It seemed unfair. *Wasn't I just as good or a better skier than the two of them?* Earlier in the afternoon, my ski instructor had said I'd skied well in class but I needed to learn to slow down and glide with a continuous motion. *Was I being held back for going too fast?* For the next several weeks, I worked hard to follow right behind the instructor, learning to slow down and only going as fast as the slowest person. We were a unit and a family.

Then to my surprise, a week or two later, I heard the words I'd been waiting for. "You look like you need more of a challenge," the ski instructor said with a smile as he sat beside me on an outdoor bench and we removed out ski boots. "Are you ready to advance to an intermediate class?" he asked.

Tilting my head to one side, I looked into his tanned, weather-beaten face and giving him a nod, I answered, "I'm ready."

In February, it sometimes rained on a day when we were supposed to ski. On those days, our skiing lesson was postponed to another day and we instead had a language lesson.

Along with our morning greeting, before each class my new ski instructor spoke to us for ten minutes about safety on the slopes. He warned us that most skiers became lost or injured during their last run of the day. Fatigued, a skier was in danger of willingly pushing themselves beyond their skills, or simply being careless and not paying attention to the snow conditions. He emphasized how important it was for us to remain in our group and always ski in pairs. Listening to his warning, I paid attention, understanding the significance of his words.

It was our last run for the day on my seventh lesson with my new instructor. I stood in line with my classmates at the summit. The instructions were to ski one behind the other, staying close together, and play follow-the-leader to the bottom of the mountain.

It was four o'clock. Glancing around, I noticed that the setting sun had grown dimmer and that the fog enshrouding the peak was rolling down the mountain. It was impossible to distinguish the snow from the sky.

With our instructor going first, we skied one behind the other, snaking our way, twisting and turning down the trail to the bottom of the ski hill. Last in line and bringing up the rear, I couldn't see anyone's colored anorak in front of me. Recalling the instructor's warnings about the last run of the day as my ski class disappeared out of sight, I worried, "What if I fell or lost my balance and skied out of bounds? Who would find me in this fog?"

The white became whiter as I inched my way forward, watching for ski tracks in the snow. I couldn't tell where the mountain ended and the fog began. My classmates didn't know that I couldn't keep up with them. I wanted to cry, but didn't. Instead, I thought of a familiar happy Walt Disney song I liked and sang it aloud. The clarity of my singing voice calmed my thoughts and my nervousness. I told myself, don't worry. You'll be alright. You'll make it down in one piece. Then my worst nightmare happened.

In my attempt to catch up with the group, I skied too fast, and lost control when I hit an icy patch. Like a luge, my skis became faster until I hit deeper snow and wiped out. I fell down into a tangled mess with snow above and below me, my skis criss-crossed, my right ski harness unbuckled, and my ankle hurting like it was sprained. It was a moment in my life, although lasting much longer than a moment, when sadness, injury and misery gobbled me up. I knew there was no way I'd catch up to the others. They'd all gone on without me.

Using my ski poles for support, I stood up, fastened my skies to my ski boots and slowly stepped my way up to where I'd flown off the trail. It was at least forty-five minutes before I exited the dense fog and saw brighter daylight.

I was thrilled at the sight before my eyes when I spotted my class waiting and watching for me at the bottom of the ski-run. I had made it. The familiar sound of their voices settled my nerves. The sight of their faces warmed my heart. I could breathe again as the tension drained from my muscles. "Phew!" I sighed, feeling relieved. My ankle was swollen and sprained, but would heal with time. My injuries could have been a lot worse. That ski experience was one I'd never forget and one I hoped never to repeat.

Spring skiing attracted many tourists. They flocked to the ski slopes with their fancy outfits, clunky ski boots and dark sunglasses ready to tan and bathe in the warmth over two hour lunches of sandwiches and pints of beer. Peach blossoms and pink snow against a sapphire sky sparkled in the sunlight. Lineups for the chairlift grew longer and wider. As our ski class would add to the congestion, we were permitted to ski without an instructor as long as we didn't ski alone.

One day, a new girl who was less familiar with the slopes asked if she could ski with me. Her name was Andrea and she was from Saint-Gervais, France. When she said, "Is it okay if I ski with you? I want to learn your style," I felt flattered. Happy to have a ski companion, I answered, "Yes, of course."

Andrea and I got on well. We enjoyed each other's sense of humor and adventuresome attitude. And we both liked European food.

With clear sunny skies and fresh snow, it was a perfect morning. Leading the way from the top of the hill to the bottom and back to the chairlift, I demonstrated my style. Like a ski instructor, skies aligned side by side, I parallel skied across moguls. Using the hill for momentum, Andrea and I zigzagged down the mountain. Not an easy skill to master, we both fell many times, laughing each time we tumbled. By midday, we had enjoyed several runs and were sad when it was time to join our classmates for lunch at our designated meeting place on the patio in front of the ski lodge. Being Andrea's personal ski instructor touched my heart.

That was the only time Andrea and I skied together. The weather changed, and cloudbursts, thunder and sudden downpours made it impossible to enjoy time on the slopes. Warmer temperatures turned the snow to liquid, and the sun evaporated our blanket of fun. Exposed to the spring sunshine, the brown grass grew greener and greener. April showers pitter-pattered on the chalet windows. Unhappy and discontented, I begrudgingly accepted that the ski season had ended. It was back to studies and final exams. Soon, new students would be arriving to begin the May to August summer semester. As it was my third term, I was expected to stay for further language classes and water skiing lessons on the lake.

Before breakfast on the first Sunday in May, I laid in bed propped up on pillows. The curtains were drawn open and sunlight streamed into my room as I listened to cow bells in the distance. As the cows leisurely sauntered towards the chalet, the sound of their swaying bells grew louder. It was the neighborhood May Day Festival. When I heard yodeling outside my window, I jumped up and looked outside. Singing in harmony, the local voices blended together as if they were one.

Everyone seemed to be enjoying their unhurried stroll along the gravel path. Dozens of families were walking behind their respective herd. The men and boys were dressed in traditional

Swiss lederhosen. The women and girls wore colorful dresses with white aprons. They were shepherding their cattle five-thousand feet up the mountain to greener pastures for the summer months. The proud families had decorated their livestock with brightly colored flags. Garland wreaths of spring flowers hung around each cow's neck, and bigger than usual, heavy brass cowbells resounded with every movement. Apparently, the lead cow with the biggest wreath, the most flowers, and the heaviest bell had produced the highest quality of milk for making Emmental cheese, a locally hand-churned hard Swiss Cheese with holes in it.

That evening would also be our final Sunday restaurant dinner together. Like the cows, many of my friends were leaving for greener pastures. Moe was flying to London the next day. Andrea was leaving for Paris where she'd enrolled in a six-month chef's Cordon Blue cuisine cooking school. Wishing I could do the same, I felt over-the-moon envious. I would have loved to spend six months in Paris. Our good-bye dinner would celebrate the end of the term and a new beginning for each of us.

Coinciding with the scattering of friends who felt like family, three letters from my boyfriend arrived together. In each letter, he professed his love and urged me to come home. Feeling nostalgic about my parting friends, missing my boyfriend, and wanting to leave for greener pastures too, I phoned my parents. While speaking with Mom, I told her that I wanted to skip the summer semester. I was finished with the international school. She understood and said that I could come home early.

Following our dinner, my roommates and I sat together in the chalet family room and chatted until midnight. It was our final girly-girl night. Sitting cross-legged, I leaned back in the large, overstuffed lounge chair, and silently listened to their chatter as

I watched their laughing, frowning, nodding animated faces. Saying good-bye was rough. I'd miss their faces and playful giggles.

After about an hour and a half sleep, long before dawn, I got up to wish Huckleberry a final farewell. She was leaving for South Africa. Outwardly, we excitedly talked about our future hopes and dreams. Inwardly, knowing that I'd probably never see her again, I was sad.

When Principal learned I'd be leaving early, she called me into her office. During our conversation, she told me that I'd matured and developed into a polite, friendly individual. I assumed she was referring to how I had overcome my shyness, and fear of speaking two foreign languages. She also said that she was pleased that I'd passed my A-level examinations. I giggled. It was great news as I'd been worried that I might not have passed. She went on to say that I'd grown in many ways. No matter how big the obstacle appeared in front of me, I'd often find a way to rise above it. Sensitive to her kind words, I walked out of her office in happy tears. Until that conversation, I had no idea that she saw me as a strong, independent and capable person.

Once everybody left, the chalet fell eerily silent. It was three days before I'd fly to Canada. During the little time I had left, Heidi and I walked the familiar stone path to Interlaken. I shopped for gifts to take home, bought an Air Canada ticket, and arranged for my steamer trunk to be picked up. I loved Switzerland and wondered if leaving was the right choice. In an attempt to soothe my sadness, on my last day, I went into the local cafe for a final ice coffee and a slice of *fresh* Black Forest cake. I savored each delicious mouthful.

The next afternoon, Principal picked me up and drove me to the airport. Knowing she only offered to make the two-hour drive for students that she liked, I felt flattered. When she dropped me off at the airport and said, “Auf Wiedersehen,” I confidently said good-bye to her in German.

I caught the five-forty-five Air Canada direct flight to Vancouver, British Columbia. A Swiss chap seated next to me didn’t speak or understand English. While we were conversing in German, he said that he was immigrating to Canada. I told him I was going home, and that he'd love British Columbia because it was similar to Switzerland with beautiful mountains and lots of lakes.

While we chatted, I realized that the challenges he was about to face were similar to the one’s I’d left behind. Like me, it was brave of him to travel to a new country where he didn't speak the language. It seemed serendipitous that nine months later, my seat mate's journey was taking him along a similar path as mine, but in the opposite direction. I wondered if his being seated next to me was a mere coincidence or if the universe had intervened. *Had the angels that be found a way to reflect my life? Had I been shown a mirror image of myself as a demonstration of my personal growth?*

Glancing out my tiny cabin window, I marveled at the orange glow of the continual setting sun as we flew in a westerly direction across Canada. When we were over the Rockies, I pointed out the snowcapped mountains to the Swiss chap. In the air for twelve hours, we landed in Vancouver where I said good-bye to my seat mate and caught a flight to Victoria, my hometown.

Waking up in Switzerland one morning, and landing in Canada the next seemed surreal. Expecting to be greeted by my boyfriend, I was shocked to see my family instead of him. However, I was delighted that my mom, dad, sister, and aunt had all come to welcome me home. I guess they missed me. They’d even planned a homecoming dinner party in my honor for that evening. It didn't take me long to realize that my boyfriend hadn't been invited.

During the drive into town from the airport, I noticed a number of unfamiliar buildings, including a new commercial mall being constructed. Some street sign names had changed and a new highway interchange had been built. Jet lag and the unanticipated changes made me feel as though I'd been away for much longer than nine months. I felt like a stranger in my hometown, which magnified the continual refrain in my mind: "Who am I and where do I belong?"

The evening dinner party was extraordinary. We feasted on smoked salmon and drank red wine. I shared stories of my experiences at the international school, entertaining my family with tales of what my chalet roommates and I had done, and how Principal had given me a glowing final report. After dinner, we exchanged gifts. I presented them with Swiss souvenirs, and they gave me household items. Apparently, they expected that I'd soon be moving out of our family home. In their eyes, I'd come of age.

Unfortunately for my boyfriend, absence hadn't made my heart grow fonder; it had made me grow stronger. I was more independent and determined to live life in accordance with my dreams and ambitions. Throughout the summer, the more he pursued our getting married, the more imprisoned I felt. Within a few months of my return, I broke up with him. He seemed to be seeking a mother rather than a wife.

The wise words of my Swiss ski instructor kept coming to mind. "Verboten! Zu Schnell." His caution to slow down was in reference to my fearlessness on the mountain. But it applied to my life too. I didn't need to race ahead and accept a marriage proposal. If I did, I'd stumble and fall. I was nineteen years old.

Time was on my side. Marriage and children could wait until after I built a career. In the meantime, I'd follow my heart. Despite what my ex-boyfriend wanted, and what my parents advised, I knew what path was best for me.

As my gap year drew to a close, my hopes, dreams, ambitions and aspirations came to fruition. Focused on my future, I registered as a freshman at the University of Victoria. By mid-September, I'd joined the university ski team and was exercising daily to get in shape for the new snow season. A month later, I met a dark-haired young man and fellow skier who was proud of his Austrian roots. The German I'd learned at school came in handy when speaking to his family.

It was by staying on my path and not skiing out of the bounds of my heart, that I came out of the fog. I knew who I was and where I belonged. The view from my self-directed mountaintop shone brightly as my soul's light expanded.

About Josephine Lavallee

Josephine Lavallee lives in South Surrey, British Columbia. She has a B.A. from the University of Victoria and a 5th year Teaching Certificate in Primary Education from the University of British Columbia.

Josephine is a member of the Great Vancouver Writers Association and past-president of the Vancouver

Island Chapter of the Romance Writers of America. Her published works include the chapter's newsletter, the B.C. Kindergarten Curriculum Guide for Correspondence Schools, and poetry. Her work in progress is a mystery novel.

Her chapter, "I'm No Dummy," in *Heartmind Wisdom #2* (an inspirational anthology with 21 authors' journeys of triumph) is a heartwarming and inspiring account of what it's like to be labeled a slow learner by grade-school teachers. Unfortunately for Josephine, she wasn't diagnosed dyslexic until she left the traditional education system. Through incredible coping skills, determination, and an unshakable belief in her abilities, she eventually proved to her naysayers that they were mistaken about her potential.

Having extensively studied the art of fiction and nonfiction writing and passionate about helping others, Josephine regularly mentors aspiring authors. A storyteller by nature, she writes and recites tales for adults and children.

She has traveled extensively, including backpacking around Europe and skiing in Switzerland. Her ambition is to live part-time on the Hawaiian Islands. She enjoys cooking elaborate dinners, reading, water sports, and jigsaw puzzles.

Connect with Josephine Lavallee
E-Mail: josephine.lavallee@gmail.com
Facebook: www.facebook.com/josephine.lavallee.7

Journey #9

MORE THAN AN INCH

Joyce (Joy) M. Ross

Kneeling in front of an overstuffed living room chair, I bellowed down the hall for the umpteenth time, "I wanna see Nana!"

"Well, you can't. Children aren't allowed in the hospital." Standing in front of the bathroom mirror, Mom puckered her lips and kissed a Kleenex.

Flopping my face into the cushion, I went back to screaming throat-stinging loud and pounding the seat of the armchair with my fists as I thumped the tops of my feet against the hardwood floor. All of me hurt. But I didn't care. I had to see Nana.

"Why do you want to see Nana so badly?" my mother asked, alerting me that she was now standing next to me and what my siblings and I referred to as the *duck* chair.

Thinking there was a chance I'd get to see Nana, I glanced up, wiped at my tears, and went mute. I had no idea *why* I had to see Nana.

Mom collected a photo of our family that was tucked into a frame that had a tiny plastic fern on one side and resembled a rather slim aquarium minus the fish. After kissing each of us kids on the head, she left.

Sadder than I'd ever before been, I got off the floor and curled up in the overstuffed armchair that Mom had recovered in a material adorned with the mallard ducks Dad claimed were *good eatin'*. My eyes burned like there was soap in them, my ankles ached like I'd been skating in wrong-sized skates all day, and my red, swollen fists throbbed like my heart had jumped half in each one and was trying to get out so it could mend itself back together like Humpty Dumpty.

Nana died the next day.

When I was nine years old, my father lost his boat building business as a result of the crooked actions of his so-called partner. My parents sold the three-bedroom house Dad had built on Lake Nipissing in North Bay, Ontario, and moved our brood to the outskirts of Victoria on Vancouver Island, British Columbia.

Far less than rich, the six of us moved into a well-ventilated shack with one decent-sized bedroom and one walk-in-closet-sized bedroom. We three girls got the big room. My brother slept on a sofa bed in the living room. Mom and Dad made do with the closet.

Though my older sister and I took turns picking fights with and trading pals, as the years rolled by, Crystal was the neighborhood friend I valued most. She had mesmerizing green eyes the size of chestnuts and shoulder-length curly hair like Shirley Temple's. I'm not sure why I liked her best, I just did.

The weird thing about Crystal was that her family lived in a small apartment that was attached to the funeral parlor where her dad worked as the director. As soon as she could do so without us getting caught, she took me downstairs to the dimly-lit, gray-walled showroom where a couple of dozen satin-lined coffins were waiting, lids open, for someone to sleep in them for eternity. They looked comfy enough, but I couldn't decide which would suit me best. Maybe the one lined with blue satin; blue was my favorite color.

When we met, though I knew about death because Nana had died and because our dog Mike had been put to sleep after he got a bone lodged in his throat and no one could get it out, I wasn't entirely certain what death was all about. One thing that I did know for sure was that eventually whomever or whatever you loved went somewhere forever, maybe Heaven.

Mom and Dad did their best to help us kids understand that dying wasn't necessarily a bad thing, which was why Heaven was only a *possible* final destination. Mom was raised Catholic and occasionally mentioned some places called hell and purgatory, where you didn't want to go but would if you misbehaved too much. Then there was the whole business of Armageddon and judgment day that I learned about at a Saturday afternoon Jehovah's Witnesses Bible school picnic.

I went to the picnic because Mom wanted us to learn about different religions, and because I thought it'd be fun. Which it was, except for the scalding sun beaming down on my hatless head and the foaming dark-brown liquid with bits of white stuff floating around in it that they served in a tall glass at lunch. Certain it had either gone bad or was poison, even when the other kids drank theirs, there was no way I was gonna drink mine. When I later told Mom about it, she said it was an ice-cream float.

As President John F. Kennedy had been shot and killed by a maniac when I was seven years old, I also knew that no matter how famous or important you were, there was no escaping this trip to *Never, Never Want To Go There Land.* At the time, I was in grade two and had made friends with a classmate who'd emigrated from the United States. We were both too young to fully understand the significance of the tragedy, but that didn't stop her from crying when our teacher told us about it.

For the next several days, everyone talked about how sad it was that the U.S. President had been shot. People felt bad for his wife and kids. Even the man who lived inside our radio was upset and talked about it a lot. We didn't have a television, but if the pictures on the front page of the *North Bay Nugget* were an indicator, the people in *TV Land* were probably sad too.

When preteen age, after the nice lady I was babysitting for was killed in a car crash, fear of dying settled into my gut like a bunch of glued-together rocks. Two doors away from our home, the woman and her family lived in the nicest and biggest house of the five that made up what my older sister and I had dubbed *the boondocks*. On that ill-fated day, the woman planned to leave at 7:00 a.m. to drive up the island to visit friends, and then drive back down in time to watch the local stock car races at Western Speedway.

As her mom was about to go out the door that morning, crying and screeching, her youngest, a toddler, wrapped her pudgy little arms around her mom's legs and clung on. Her mother and I were shocked. I enjoyed babysitting the little girl, and she seemed to like me. Her mother often went out, so neither the woman nor I could figure out why the little girl was suddenly so upset. When her mother closed the door and left, the toddler collapsed on the floor and sobbed and sobbed.

Two hours later, I called her uncle and asked him to come over and help me calm her down. He couldn't quiet his niece. When he tried to pick her up, like she had with me, she flailed her arms and screamed. Eventually, the poor little dickens fell asleep on the floor and we put her to bed.

When her mom didn't come home at 11:00 p.m., I called the same uncle and asked him to spend the night with his niece so I could go home. We received the bad news early the next morning. The nice lady had been killed in a car accident on her way back down the island. Apparently, a drunk driver had swerved into her lane and hit her car head-on. The impact caused the steering wheel to snap in half and pierce her heart. I cried for hours. Everyone in the boondocks was sad for weeks.

By then, I'd learned about reincarnation. Upset about the nice lady's death and acutely aware of life's unpredictability, I spent numerous hours trying to decide what living creature I'd like to be on my next trip to earth. At first, I was partial to becoming an evergreen tree like the ones that towered over the golf course across the street from our house. Trees lived for hundreds of years and got to play outside day and night. Equally fascinating was that they could see for miles. I knew this because I'd once scurried up the branches of a cloud-tall pine until I was so high that my friends below appeared tinier than Crystal's hamster's pencil-eraser-sized pink and hairless babies. Going up the branches was hurry-up-and-get-there fun; coming down was take-your-time, heart-trying-to-thump-its-way-out-of-your-rib-cage scary.

When it dawned on me that trees were stationary, I decided to reincarnate as a seagull. Gulls could fly and liked junk food as much as I did. It sometimes took me years to catch on, so by then I had a job, my own place, and a couple of new best friends—Patricia and Patricia. To ensure they both didn't answer when I asked a question, I called them by their nicknames, Patti and Trish.

To make sure that God, or whoever put the stamp of approval on one's passport back to earth, was hyperaware of my decision to reincarnate as a seagull, when I was visiting the store where Trish worked and spotted a gigantic framed picture of a gull flying high in a brilliant blue sky, I bought it and hung it on a wall in my apartment.

Patti, Trish and I weren't angels. Beginning with thinking it was a ton of fun to help the teenage boys from the Belmont Park navy housing complex turn over their neighbors' garbage cans, and ending with underage drinking, we were brats. In between, there were games of spin-the-bottle and truth-or-dare where we took turns kissing each of the Belmont Park boys.

Like most teenagers, we took a lot of dumb risks. We hitch-hiked and let friends drive us around when they were stoned or drunk. During the summertime, we snuck out late at night to smoke cigarettes on the pitch-black golf course. All three of us survived, but not all of our friends and family did.

Rick from the navy housing complex died in a car crash. Sharon, one of our friends at Elizabeth Fisher Junior High School, rolled her car off the highway, landed upside down in a ditch, and drowned. Patti's dad got sick and passed away. A few years later, her mom died from cancer.

From 1974 to 1980, I worked with troubled teens at the Victoria Youth Detention Centre. During the six years I worked there, at different times after they were released back into society, about a half-dozen teens who'd spent time in the center were killed in car accidents or committed suicide.

Beginning with Nana, each death broke my heart. They were all good people worthy of a spot in Heaven. They were all deeply loved, and their families and close friends would miss them for a long time. But not the rest of the world.

Unlike when President J. F. Kennedy was assassinated, following each of their deaths, there were no radio or television reports, no newspaper headlines, no lengthy write-ups about the contributions each had made to society. Instead, buried toward the back of the local paper, each one's life was marked with an inch-long announcement that included the dates of his or her birth and death, the names of immediate relatives, and the location of the funeral service.

When young and there forward, I viewed this inequality as an injustice. How could one person's life be less important than another's? Dead or alive, why did the media celebrate one being and not another? Everyone deserved to have his or her contributions recognized, rejoiced and remembered. Newspaper-wise, the space needed to properly honor each one was far more than an inch.

After I quit the detention center, I moved to Toronto, Ontario, where my older sister was studying law. During a discussion with my Aunt Nina about my having to find a job or go back to school, she asked, "What do you want to do for a living?" Without forethought, "I want to be a writer!" popped out of my mouth, surprising her and me.

After reading a zillion *True Romance* magazines, at age fourteen, I had penned a short story and sent it off to the publisher. Crafting poetry was delightful child's play, and I'd enjoyed studying English in school. Past that, I wasn't consciously aware that I wanted to be a writer. Obviously, my subconscious had been keeping secrets from me. Either that, or an extraterrestrial being had been flying overhead on its way somewhere and overheard my conversation with Aunt Nina. When she asked her question, it chose a random card out of the earthly occupations deck it kept in its bag of fool-the-humans tricks and slotted it into my brain. Regardless, my mind and soul were aboard the become-a-writer ship that set sail in my heart.

Over the next year, I lived off savings and diligently worked at becoming a romance novelist. My first manuscript off to Harlequin, I banged out a second one on the old Olivetti electric typewriter that once belonged to my mother. Bottles of liquid White Out and reams of paper consumed my budget while writing consumed me.

The next year, I took a part-time job as a cocktail waitress at Peter's Backyard restaurant and bar. During the day, I wrote. Evenings and nights, I carried trays of drinks over my head as I smiled and excused my way through a packed room of partiers. When Harlequin rejected my first novel, I pouted in bed for a couple of days; when they rejected the second, I quit writing.

After my sister completed law school, the two of us moved to Vancouver, British Columbia. A waitress I worked with at the Bayshore Hotel introduced me to the Mary Kay Cosmetics business opportunity. Shortly after achieving pink-car status, my sister and I started marketing non-run hosiery via our own direct sales company. After a few years, she returned to practicing law, and three new partners and I expanded the home party-plan business across North America. Year six, Pelican Publishing purchased the rights to my book *Direct Sales: Be Better Than Good–Be Great!* Year eight, we sold the business and I started running singles dances for the over-forty crowd.

For the next fourteen years, I earned a decent living organizing bands and venues for Saturday night dances. It was a ton of fun, and I thoroughly got a kick out of telling people that I partied for a living. Having had my how-to book published, my ego recovered from Harlequin's rejection of my manuscripts, so between organizing and partying, I resumed writing romance.

My yearning to become a romance novelist wasn't all that followed me into that career. Much like my work at the youth detention center, people I cared about died one after another. Stomach cancer took Rob and his contagious laugh into the next world, where I'm positive he's still making jokes that send his fellow deceased into hysterics.

Like nobody else, Rob could poke fun at someone so that they saw the humor in their own flaws and laughed. His ribbing of me came with actual pokes. Often, he'd sneak up behind me, lightly poke both sides of my waist and call me *spongy*.

One day when a bunch of us were on a packed Skytrain headed into Vancouver, Rob jumped up at a scheduled stop, and in a deep voice announced, "Everybody off!" Most of the non-singles-club passengers stood up and prepared to exit. Those of us who knew him roared with laughter. Everyone sat back down.

Rob met Susan at a club function. Except for their height and attractive facial features, at first consideration, they were opposites. She had thick, long brown hair; his hair was thinned and short. He was gregarious and outgoing; she was shy and introverted. What they did have in common was lots of children and a love of wrestling each other. At least it seemed that way when a bunch of us spent a weekend at a lodge near Squamish, B.C. I still chuckle when I look at the photo of the two of them on the floor, wearing pajamas, each with the other in a leg-lock as they killed themselves laughing.

A couple of years in a row, about two dozen of us headed to Harrison Hot Springs for a camping trip. As the organizer, I chose that area because Harrison Lake is beautiful, and if we didn't feel like cooking, we could eat at one of the nearby restaurants.

One night, after a few of us had snuck off to a local bar for drinks and dancing, I went back to the campsite early and tucked Susan's kids into their sleeping bags. About two hours later, I heard Rob and Susan outside the tent. She hated camping and in her drunken state was refusing to crawl into their tent in case there were bugs in there.

As Susan and Rob weren't big drinkers, the next morning, I

teased her about having had a few too many. Laughing, she shared how as she and Rob staggered back to camp, the police had stopped them and asked if they were planning on driving. Rob responded, "I can hardly walk. How the heck would I drive a car?"

A couple of weeks before he died, Rob invited his closest friends from our club to his and Susan's place. He'd appeared frail and skinny. "Hey," he said as we walked through the door. "Don't I look great! My Jenny Craig diet's working wonders for me."

Within a few short years, cancer claimed Arnold, Arnie, Gil, Jeannie, and more. Steve's love of beer was what got him. Wally's heart gave out while he was playing ice hockey. Eugene, a dear friend and my roommate, had a heart attack and died in our backyard.

When Eugene died, I wrote a short story about him and gave copies to the dozens of grief-stricken friends at his standing-room-only funeral. One of the kindest people to ever grace the earth, Eugene loved to make people happy.

One day, I spotted him washing his fancy red convertible while wearing a clown outfit. "Why are you dressed that way?" I asked, a chuckle in my belly. "I want to make people laugh," was his reply. I nodded and left him alone to continue his mission.

Eugene feared death, so we often talked about our beliefs regarding the afterlife. During more than one heart-to-heart, we promised each other that, provided it was possible, the first to die would come back to tell the other about eternity. Forever a loyal friend, Eugene kept his promise.

A few months after he died, Eugene appeared in my dream to warn me not to make a residence change I'd been contemplating. In the dream, we were sitting on a bench in the forest exchanging telepathic thoughts about missing each other. After a while, Eugene stood and walked toward a part in a thick hedge. "Wait, wait," I hollered. "You promised to tell me what it's like to be dead." Eugene looked back toward me, a sweet smile on his peaceful face as he said, "It's really nice."

The next day, I told my friend Patricia about my dream. After I shared that Eugene had left my dream through a part in a hedge, she asked, "Where were you?" It was an odd question, but one I was certain had a purpose.

"We were sitting on a bench in a forest," I answered.

"His soul must have truly visited you," Patricia said. "When I was counseling Eugene for anxiety, his safe place was a bench in the forest."

Though I continued to sometimes dream about Eugene, and said hello when he often came to mind, he never again visited my dream in spirit-form.

It was years before I realized the connection between my childhood tantrum when I couldn't see Nana and the young tyke's tantrum when her mother left for the day and the little girl somehow knew that her mom was never coming back. Evidently, children are more in tune with their spiritual knowings than most adults.

Eugene is one of many deceased beings that have made their wishes, regrets, and thoughts known to me. If we were all more aware and certain of our everlasting soul-to-soul connections with departed loved ones, though we'd still miss them in the physical world, there'd be far fewer tears shed when people we care about return to the spirit world.

Having lost countless friends and a few family members to the eternal side, one summer evening about two years ago, I sat in the backyard saying hello to one spirit pal after the other. For more than a half hour, memories surfaced as familiar faces floated before my mind's eye. When I couldn't recall any more departed chums, feeling melancholic, I stared into the darkening sky. It was then that a drop of water fell into the corner of my right eye. Startled, I glanced up at the tall evergreen overhead. The tree was crying for me; the Universe was letting me know that my loved ones were nearby.

As an inspirational author, it warms my heart that ages from now, when someone reads about my friends and family, my loved ones' spirits will echo forward. I also edit and publish inspirational stories. Helping others craft their literary legacies affords me absolute joy. Every morning, seven days a week, it's my privilege to awake before dawn, throw on a pot of coffee, and then spend numerous hours absorbed in my own or someone else's life-gained wisdom. It also warms my soul, that like me, one story at a time, authors around the globe are honoring their own and others' lives with far more than an inch.

About Joyce (Joy) M. Ross

Joyce (Joy) M. Ross is the publisher of the Heartmind Wisdom Collection and the Earth Angels Series. She is also the creator of the Heartmind Store which connects readers and writers in a deeper, more meaningful way. On a mission to revolutionize how authors are trained, promoted and compensated, she also created the Empowered Author Self-Publishing Course.

Her chapter in *Heartmind Wisdom Collection #1* is "Rainbows, Butterflies and Other Miracles," and her chapter in *Heartmind Wisdom Collection #2* is "Taming Shame & Blame." This story, "More Than an Inch," was originally published in *Heartmind Wisdom Collection #3*. Joyce's published works include *The Kindness Ambassador* and *Direct Sales: Be Better than Good – Be Great!*

Connect with Joyce (Joy) M. Ross
E-Mail: joy_ross@hotmail.com
Website: www.heartmindstore.com
Facebook: www.facebook.com/WritingWithJOY

Journey #10

A SPIRITUAL FAREWELL WITH DADDY

Karen Reidie-Thorstad

It was June 21st, 1975. My husband, Doug, and I were out on our boat fishing in Finlayson Arm on Vancouver Island. At exactly one o'clock, the song "My Way" by Frank Sinatra came on radio. An overwhelming feeling of deep loss came over me. As if it were an omen, like the title of the song, Dad always did things *his way*. My eyes welled with tears.

"I think something just happened to Daddy," I said.

"Do you want go in?" Doug asked.

An unexpected feeling of serenity came over me, and I was aware of Daddy's presence. Having suffered two massive cerebral hemorrhages, my father had been hospitalized for the past nine months. The left side of his body was totally paralyzed, and he couldn't speak. I had witnessed his frustration and anguish many times and could feel that he was now at peace.

Answering my husband's question, I said, "No, knowing Daddy, I don't think he'd want us to rush in and cut our fishing trip short. I think he would want us to stay out here and enjoy the rest of the day."

"You know best," my husband said good-naturedly.

It was a beautiful, sunny day, and I found the ocean calming. After making my way to the bow, I sat at the very tip and watched white waves gently wash against the boat. For the next few hours, I thought about my father and all the things he'd done his way.

My dad was a machinist with the Canadian Pacific Railway. A shift-worker, he often worked all night. When the train he serviced was on a run, he fabricated and repaired train parts on a metal lathe. To keep himself busy, when he ran out of work-related projects, he'd experiment on ones of his own.

Dad had a lapel pin that he'd received for service in the Canadian army during the Second World War. Forever creative, he fashioned a small stainless steel heart on the lathe. He then embedded the lapel pin into the heart and presented the pendant to Mom on a sterling silver chain. She wore her necklace with pride for many years.

One day, he came home with a wooden baseball bat he'd made for me. I was ecstatic. I'd always wanted to learn how to play the game. It wasn't long before I broke the bat in half, and the next three didn't withstand hitting a ball either. Dad was a man of patience, but when I told him about the fourth broken bat, he finally gave up. "I guess you can't make a wooden bat on a metal lathe," was all he said.

Mom and Dad were married in 1927, and my brother was born in 1930. It was a shock to my parents when sixteen years later, mom learned she was pregnant with me. She was thirty-nine and my dad was forty-one. Having more children wasn't in their plans. On June 27th, 1946, I entered the world healthy, and weighing seven pounds, six ounces. Apparently, my arrival was much to the chagrin of my teenage brother. He quit school and joined the circus shortly after I was born. In those days, few women had babies in their late thirties, and sixteen years between children wasn't the norm. Many times, Mom explained the disparity in our ages as me being an "afterthought."

"Sugar and spice and everything nice, that's what little girls are made of." I'm not sure I fit into that category; still, I always knew I was "Daddy's girl."

One of my favorite childhood memories was when my dad came home with a tricycle on my fourth birthday. He taught me how to attach a baseball card to a wheel spoke using a wooden clothes peg. It made a cool clicking sound, and the faster I peddled, the louder the clicking became. Shy by nature, when all the kids in the neighborhood copied me, I was surprised, happy, and suddenly popular. On my ninth birthday, he surprised me again with my first two-wheel bicycle. I'd never been on a big-kids' bike. Dad ran alongside me with his hand on the seat to balance me as I pedaled. His perseverance outweighed my frustration by a longshot. I eventually got the hang of it, and cycling became a passion.

My mom, being a bit of a gypsy, liked to change residences every year. Over a dozen years, that meant twelve different schools for me. I hated it. As if to soften the blow of yet another new school, my dad made a swing for me in every basement and hung one in every backyard of every new house. I swung on my swing and sang songs for hours on end.

Mom and Dad often attended dances and other functions at the local legion where they were members. One day, they brought home a song book for me. Having heard many of the songs on the radio and on Mom's record player, I was familiar with the tunes and most of the words. When I couldn't understand the lyrics, I would substitute whatever words sounded close. The song "So Long, It's Been Good to Know Ya" by the Weavers became "So long, roll out the linoleum." Perhaps that's why they brought home the song book. But maybe not, as I often caught Daddy smiling to himself as I sang. I think he actually got a kick out of hearing me sing the wrong words.

I loved movies, especially westerns. Every Saturday afternoon, I would go to the theater, even if I had to go by myself. Mom gave me a weekly allowance for the small chores I did around the house. Just before I'd walked out the door, Daddy would slip me whatever change he had in his pocket.

Figure skating was the only activity I enjoyed more than riding my bike and going to movies. During the winter months when we lived in Edmonton, Alberta, I skated for hours on end at outdoor rinks. My parents recognized my potential and scraped together enough money for lessons. When I was eleven, I earned a silver medal from our local figure skating club. When Daddy was transferred to Victoria, British Columbia, the milder winters were not conducive to outdoor skating rinks. Figure skating lessons were more expensive than they had been in Alberta. After a few months, my parents said they could no longer afford them. From then on, my favorite activity was limited to public skating rinks. Friday, Saturday and Sunday, my friends and I spent as much time as possible on the ice.

When Friday night skating ended at eleven o'clock, I'd call my dad for a ride home. Never once did he complain about the two or three friends I asked him to drop off on our way. He never wanted me to catch a bus or walk home in the dark, saying, "I don't want the bogeyman to get you." It was an often repeated caution that helped to keep me safe and resulted in me being afraid of the dark forever.

I never expected my dad to be at my beck and call, but I always knew I could count on him. When things went awry, Daddy was ready to right them. One day, a bus driver pulled into my stop, waited for me to get to the doors, and then closed them and drove away. Astounded and upset, I ran home in tears, afraid that I would be late for work. Visibly upset too, my dad drove me to work, consoling me along the way. He couldn't believe anyone would mistreat another that way.

Mom was the disciplinarian in the family. In those days, misbehaved boys got the belt, and girls got the "bad girl" stick or were grounded. I got the hairbrush, but only once. Mom broke it over my derriere. I think Mom felt worse than my stinging backside because she never hit me again. I can't recall what I'd done that was so bad, but it was during Mom's menopausal days. Daddy only hit me once, and I remember it like it was yesterday.

I was fifteen years old, and in my room suffering with horrible cramps and nausea. I was lying on the bed moaning when Mom called me to dinner. Not well enough to get up, I hollered out that I didn't feel well and couldn't eat. Dad arrived at my closed bedroom door a few seconds later. He said that Mom had gone to a lot of trouble making a nice roast beef dinner, and that I should come to the table.

I was insistent that I couldn't make it. He started to get very angry. Having never seen that side of him before, I was unnerved. I quickly got up and locked my door. That infuriated him. The situation might not have escalated the way it did if he hadn't used a ladder to climb up the back of the house to get to my bedroom window. The house was older and had wood-framed windows that opened upward. I was on my bed, legs crossed, arms locked over my chest when he lifted the window wide open and stuck his head through. A split-second later, the heavy window crashed down on his head.

I couldn't help myself. It struck me as being funny, and I started to laugh. Daddy's face flushed red as he slithered through the window and onto the floor, blood trickling down his forehead. Once on his feet, he stormed over and cuffed me on my left ear so hard that he knocked me off the bed and onto the floor. I jumped up and screamed at him, “Don’t you ever do that to me again!" Daddy looked shocked by what he'd done. Without saying another word, he exited my room, and left me alone for the rest of the night.

My dad never apologized for hitting me, and I never apologized for laughing when he was hurt. I wasn't afraid of my dad, and he never hit me again. Whenever I acted out, Mom's favorite expression was "Wait til your father gets home." For me, the window incident gave new meaning to her bluff. No matter how badly I misbehaved, she never ratted me out.

Some of my fondest and funniest memories of my parents are from when I was in high school. One day after classes, my parents showed up to drive me home. One of the students said to me, “Oh, I think your Gramma and Grampa are here to pick you up.” Shocked, all I said was, “Yes, I know.” I was devasted. Until that comment, I never thought of Mom and Daddy as being older than the other students' parents. They were just my parents. After that, I didn’t take any notices home for parent-teacher night or social gatherings. I didn’t want my friends to know I had older parents. But, one day I got caught.

My best friend and I were socializing with friends at lunchtime on the school grounds when the bell rang to return to class. Lo and behold, who did we run into but my mom and my best friend’s mother. My Mom said to me, “Why didn’t you tell me about the *meet and greet the mothers tea*?” I stammered something, probably a white lie. I felt hung out to dry. The gig was up.

One day, Daddy decided to show up at school sporting his new car. It was an older Nash Rambler, a horrible little cream colored car with a pink top. It smelled fishy, and I hated it. Humiliated when one of my friends discovered that mushrooms were growing inside, I never set foot in that car again. Turns out that Daddy got a great deal on the car because it had somehow ended up at the bottom of the ocean and had been hauled up by a crane. When I later told my brother's wife about the mushroom discovery, she laughed hysterically. By then, I could see the humor in the incident. But when it happened, I wanted to die.

Daddy was the person I called whenever I had a problem. I hadn't had my driver's license very long when he bought me an old Dodge four-door sedan for fifty dollars. One day, I was out in my car when the top of my foot started burning. I pulled over to the side of the road and looked to see what was causing the excruciating pain. I couldn't see anything on my sock and had no idea what to do.

There weren't any cell phones in those days, so I hobbled over to a nearby house and asked to borrow the phone to call my dad. Not far from where I was, he seemed to appear in a heartbeat. I was in terrible pain and crying fairly hard. When Daddy arrived, he had me take off my right shoe and sock. The top of my foot was red and blistered. He looked under the dashboard to see if he could figure out what had happened but couldn't see anything. Opening the hood, he discovered that battery acid had leaked out, worked its way underneath the dashboard, and dripped on my foot. It was two weeks before I could wear shoes again.

In October 1974, Mom and Dad decided to take a bus trip to

Reno, Nevada. It was their first vacation ever. They'd been gone four days when I received a frantic call from my mother. She was calling from a hospital in Klamath Falls, Oregon. Daddy had suffered a massive stroke while they were on the bus heading home. I had a tough time believing what she was telling me.

Through sobs, Mom went on to say that Daddy was paralyzed on his entire left side and couldn't stand or speak. Shaking, my mind raced as tears streamed down my cheeks. It was difficult to hear my mom so upset. Unfathomable that my dad was paralyzed. Fighting to stay calm, I told my mother that Doug and I would get there as quickly as we could.

I was dumbfounded. Even though my father was sixty-nine, he always seemed young to me. He was active, ate well, and took pride in his appearance. He stood tall and always looked smart in his dress pants and a brimmed hat. I couldn't understand how someone so healthy and alive could suddenly be incapacitated.

I asked my best friend to look after our kids, and Doug and I caught the ferry from Vancouver Island to the mainland and headed for Klamath Falls, Oregon. Only stopping to eat and take restroom breaks, we drove all night and arrived at the hospital late afternoon on Sunday. I entered my dad's hospital room, spotted him and stopped in my tracks. Shocked, I quietly stepped out of the room, turned right, and backed up against the wall to steady myself. Cupping my hand over my mouth so Mom and Daddy wouldn't hear me, I sobbed. My dad was a prisoner in his own body.

After a few minutes, I gathered myself together as best I could, and walked back into the room. The man lying in the bed was not my daddy. I hardly recognized him. The muscles on the left side of his face sagged, and the entire left side of his body was lifeless. It horrified me to see him in such a state. He looked scared. I tried desperately to hold back my tears so as not to frighten him further.

As if in slow-motion, I moved to the side of his bed. When he saw me, the right side of his mouth turned upward. I bent over and hugged him harder than I'd ever hugged him. His right arm came up and he cuddled me as he always had. I was still Daddy's little girl.

In between visits to the hospital, over the next two days, Mom, Doug and I discussed options for transporting Dad back home to Victoria. We decided to charter a small plane as it would be faster and the least detrimental to his overall health. That didn't go well at all.

My mom's brother, Captain Freddie McCall, was a famous World War I and World War II flying ace. He used to take mom flying all the time and she loved it, especially when he would do loop-de-loops in the air. Unlike Mom, Dad was not a seasoned flyer, he'd never been in an airplane. There was terror in his eyes as his stretcher was loaded into the aircraft. The saving grace was that Mom was there at his side, reassuring him all the way.

The plane arrived in Victoria safely, and Dad was transported to St. Joseph's Hospital where he stayed for two weeks. He was later transferred to the Gorge Road Hospital for rehabilitation. That would be his home for the next nine months.

Mom was there at lunch time and stayed til after dinner every day, never missing a beat. I visited with Dad almost daily, sometimes twice a day. I had two small children and was pregnant. When I couldn't get away from home, I felt guilty and worried that something might happen in my absence.

Mom and I attended the hospital's free information classes about strokes. The hardest part for both of us was when Dad would fidget. We learned that as the paralysis was limited to his left side, Daddy could see and hear us and understood everything we were saying, but he couldn't respond. He was a fully-aware prisoner in his own body.

Whenever Dad fidgeted, knowing he wanted to communicate something, we asked him questions. "Do you need to go to the bathroom?" "Are you thirsty?" "Are you hungry, Daddy?" Then, a little tear would trickle from his eye and down his cheek. Mom and I could sense his frustration and I'm certain he could sense ours. Each time this happened, I thought my heart would break. After visiting with him, I would get in my two-seater, red Volkswagen, and through tears, scream, "I want my Daddy back."

One lovely Saturday afternoon in June, a nurse helped Dad into his wheelchair, and I took him outdoors. While wheeling him around the grounds, Dad suddenly slumped over to one side. I immediately hollered for one of the nurses to come over. She nonchalantly addressed my father, said something patronizing to him, and then told me that he was fine, he was just tired. Sensing something more serious was wrong with my dad, but as I wasn't a medical professional, I didn't argue as she wheeled him back inside.

Later that evening, Mom telephoned to tell me that Dad's doctor had called with the news that my father had suffered a cerebral hemorrhage and was in a coma. I burst into tears. The massive stroke must have happened when he slouched over in his wheelchair earlier in the day.

Mom and I continued visiting him every day, talking to him, hoping he could hear us. He didn't fidget. His eyes never opened. Daddy never woke up again.

The day that Dad transitioned, when we arrived home from our fishing trip, hearing it ringing, I ran to answer the phone. It was Mom. Sobbing, after asking where Doug and I had been all day, she told me that Daddy had passed.

Crying, I softly said, "I know. It happened at one o'clock, didn't it?"

"Yes, how did you know that?" Mom asked.

I explained that when the song "My Way" came on the radio at one o'clock, I could sense Daddy was with me and was at peace. Mom was somewhat comforted that he'd found a way to let us know that he was okay.

After we hung up, I bawled like a baby, not only from grief, but also from relief. Having witnessed his frustration and tears for nine months, I knew how much my dad hated being paralyzed. His suffering was finally over.

One week later, I woke up at exactly one o'clock in the morning and spotted Daddy standing at the foot of the bed, his arms outstretched towards me. I couldn't believe my eyes. I looked over at Doug; he was fast asleep. I glanced back at the foot of our bed, and Daddy was still standing there. I rubbed my eyes, still not believing what I was seeing. Not wanting to wake him, I glanced at my still sleeping husband as I gingerly pulled the covers back on my side and quietly got out of bed. A sense of serene peace engulfed me as I walked into my dad's open arms.

"Daddy, why are you here?" I asked.

"I came for you."

"Oh, Daddy, am I going to die too?"

Dad giggled. "No, silly, but you have something to tell me."

The familiar sound of his lighthearted laugh warmed me throughout. He'd always referred to me as "silly" when I said or did something that he found humorous. I whispered into his ear,

"Well, you left before I had a chance to say good-bye and tell you how much I love you."

"I know," he said. "That's why I came." For the next several seconds he cradled me against his chest. Comforted by the familiarity of his embrace, I felt protected and happy. Although I was sorry to feel him leaving, when Daddy gradually faded out of my arms, I kept smiling.

I looked at my still sleeping husband, then slowly made my way back to bed. Not wanting to sleep, for several hours, I reveled in those precious moments with my dad, reliving the soulful purity of our spiritual farewell.

I will always remember how it felt to be held in his arms one more time. In my heart of hearts, I know Daddy is always with me. Guiding me. Loving me.

* * *

Through the years, there were many ways my dad showed his love for me. Like calling me on the phone out of the clear blue, and asking, "Can your ole man take you out for lunch?" Or running after me when I threatened to throw myself off the Gorge Road Bridge because my boyfriend of three years had broken up with me. The many times he and Mom returned from an evening out, and Dad brought me a famous Roger's chocolate, the one that looked like a cherry bomb. And in later years, after my kids were born, he and Mom would drop by with a bottle of wine to share with Doug and me. I knew it was just an excuse to see me and check in. Daddy was always kind, always thoughtful. There are lots more tales to tell about our relationship, but some have faded with age and are just glimmers of fond memories now. Treasures I covet along with our spiritual farewell.

About Karen Reidie-Thorstad

Karen Reidie-Thorstad is a retired interior designer and published author. She lives in Victoria, British Columbia with her husband, Ross Thorstad, and their boxer, Mikki. She has three children, three stepchildren, eight grandchildren, and a great-grandson. Her hobbies include long walks, bike riding, golfing, cooking, and entertaining.

To encourage others to celebrate and share their spiritual, paranormal and transformational stories, in 1994, Karen co-founded the Angels' Hope Chest chat room on the Internet. Although the site is no longer online, she continues to share her personal spiritual experiences through writing, experiences that can only be explained by divine intervention.

Karen's writings have been published in *A Cup Of Comfort: Stories That Warm Your Heart, Lift Your Spirit, And Enrich Your Life* (2001) and in *A Cup of Comfort Classic Edition: Timeless Stories That Warm Your Heart, Lift Your Spirit, And Enrich Your Life* (2007). Her story "Angel Behind the Wheel" was published in *Woman's World Magazine* (August 19, 2013).

Connect with Karen Reidie-Thorstad
E-Mail: schmidi1@shaw.ca
Facebook: https://www.facebook.com/Mikki989

Journey #11

TAMING THE INVISIBLE DRAGON

Lindsay Laycock-Pirie

It's estimated that one in four people will endure a form of debilitating emotional distress in their lifetime. For me, that distress manifested in a three-headed invisible dragon that overpowered my thoughts, well-being and life.

During the day, my preschool childhood was outwardly fairly typical. Though I was quite shy and sensitive, I interacted with other kids, played make-believe, and loved the outdoors. But at night, while most children were treated to fanciful dreams of flying or finding hidden treasures, I endured nightmares where I was part of and trapped within a brilliant blue power grid. I would awake with a high-pitched ringing in my ears and what felt like an intense electrical current surging through my veins.

Confused, scared and physically distressed, I tried to explain my nightmares and what I felt to my parents. They comforted me and took me to a doctor who determined that I did not have tinnitus. Without a treatable medical diagnosis, I was on my own to deal with the near-nightly terror of my invisible dragon.

Throughout grade school, there were many times when I felt overwhelmed by homework, excessive noise and boisterous classmates. Without any way to gauge whether everyone felt like I did, I assumed it was normal.

In my early teens, I enjoyed socializing with friends. Events always began with me feeling fabulous for a while. Then, a "strange" feeling would wash over me. Not wanting to miss out on the fun, I endured the strangeness, dealing with my anxiousness rather than running for the safety of home.

Around my late-teens, I started to experience what I later learned were panic attacks. Although I attempted to talk about these sudden onslaughts of full-blown and uncontrollable fear, I might as well have been speaking in a foreign language. No one understood. No one could offer an explanation. I was again on my own to deal with my nameless invisible dragon, a monster that attacked me at will and was growing forever stronger.

Anxiety interfered with every aspect of my life. Unable to understand, some friends withdrew. Unable to cope, I withdrew. Dreams for the future that I'd held dear dropped behind a wall of uncertainty and insecurity. If I couldn't cope, how was I going to achieve any of the great plans I had for my life? If I couldn't achieve anything worthwhile, what was the sense in trying? Cut off from the essence of who I envisioned myself becoming when I grew up, depression joined forces with anxiety, and my invisible dragon became two-headed.

I was nineteen and living on my own when my dragon morphed into a three-headed nemesis. One afternoon, needing an ingredient from the store for that evening's meal, I opened the door of the apartment and froze as a feeling of impending doom took hold of my being. Every cell in my body filled with fear. My limbs tingled and my legs became weak as my heart pounded within my constricted chest. I could barely breathe. If I left the house something dreadful would happen. Telling myself that I was being silly, I made a few more attempts to leave home, but couldn't.

From that day forward, there were many days I was unable to leave the house on my own. My boyfriend drove me to and from the home where I worked as a nanny. I avoided going out, and spent days trying to psyche myself into attending functions where my absence wasn't an option. While attempting to socialize at one of these events, it was as if I wasn't really present. People would talk and I'd try to listen, but the fear chatter in my head turned their words into gobbledygook. After the function, it would take days for me to feel somewhat calm again.

My family doctor prescribed medication that helped a little. When at home alone, I kept the blinds drawn, the door locked, and often walked laps around the inside the apartment to try and calm myself. Every waking hour of every day, I rode a roller-coaster of fear that peaked and dipped, but never ceased. I couldn't predict what each day would bring. My dragon's third head was officially diagnosed as agoraphobia. At that point, I stopped working.

Three was a crowd I would not tolerate. There had to be a way to tame the unseen beast, and it was up to me to discover what that was. I started paying attention to the correlation between what I ate and the severity of fear I felt. Sugar was a definite trigger, so I cut sweets from my diet. Exercise helped, so I became an avid runner, running around the area I lived. Running helped dispel some of the anxiety. I also went to a counsellor and found that talking helped.

Little by little, I tamed the agoraphobia head of the dragon and was able to work again. I also became more social, though I didn't overbook my activities. Panic and depression remained constant adversaries, always lurking below the surface and readied to attack. Constantly on high alert, my tolerance level was limited. It took days, sometimes weeks, for me to recover from a mild speedbump in my life.

Wanting to help others, I stopped hiding my struggles and talked openly with people about my depression and panic attacks. By being honest and authentic regarding my emotional stressors, perhaps I could make a positive difference in someone else's life. Once my mask of self-protection was removed, I told everyone, even near strangers, about what I'd been through and what helped me. Some people viewed my challenges as a burden. I saw them as more than that. More than encumbrances, my journey with anxiety, depression and agoraphobia was a gift that provided me with unique insights that could benefit others.

Life during my twenties wasn't all smooth sailing. Medication my doctor prescribed would work for a while, then I'd need a different pill. Nothing took my anxiety away completely. The attacks where I was paralyzed with fear were less frequent and came in waves that soon past. My agoraphobia somewhat under control, I enrolled in an early childhood education course at a nearby college and managed to complete the one-year program.

In 2005, I moved from Victoria, British Columbia to Quadra island. My hope was that a quieter lifestyle and small island vibe would be just what I needed.

While exercising at the local gym, I met Reid. He was a born and raised island boy who'd been travelling the world off and on for a few years. We bumped into each other again a few days later at a local pub and talked for six hours. Kind, intelligent and calm, he was refreshingly different than the guys I'd dated before.

I was happy and sad when Reid told me that he, his brothers and their dad were taking a trip to Viet Nam in two weeks so they could spend some time together before he moved to London, England. I was happy that I'd had the chance to meet him and sad that our relationship would end so quickly. I'd travelled some, as well, and admired his outgoing, spontaneous nature. Spontaneity wasn't an impulse I embraced for myself as I strived to keep my life calm and steady.

Our physical and emotional attraction mutual and strong, we were inseparable for those two weeks. Shortly before he was to leave, Reid asked me to move to England with him. Otherwise, he'd change his plans and return home so he could be with me. Madly in love and unable to imagine my life without him, I agreed to move to London. Not wanting Reid to give up his dream gave me the courage I needed to dabble in spontaneity.

He left six weeks ahead of me, travelled Vietnam with his brothers and Dad, and then went to London and rented a flat. When I arrived, each of us got a job at the same childcare center. For the next six months, our lives were blissful. Thousands of miles away from family and friends, we became each other's rock. Although I felt safe and protected when I was at home with Reid, anxiety started creeping back into my life at work. By the end of the workday, I was an anxious mess. Eventually, I had to quit my job.

Reid was incredibly understanding. I was devastated. I could control my fear level when something big was happening, but not when life was routine. The distraction and highs of a new love, city or job overpowered my fears and dulled my depression, but sneakily infiltrated my emotional well-being when the happy waters calmed.

When we moved back to Canada a year later, we got engaged. The excitement of planning our wedding reduced my fear to a simmer, and I went back to work as an educational assistant in an elementary school. It was a short-lived high followed by the inevitable crash. Once again, I quit working and went back to being trapped at home.

Reid and I married in July 2006 and moved to the Kootenays in southeastern British Columbia. Our daughter, Milly, was born in 2008. The period following Milly's birth was intense as I adjusted to hormonal changes and motherhood. I was obsessive about keep the house clean and our baby happy, safe and healthy. My mortality constantly on my mind, it took a mountain of self-convincing for me to venture outside. Like a never-ending movie, images of being in a car accident and dying continually played in my head. From morning to night, I was haunted by feelings of impending doom.

The community we lived in was remote and there was little opportunity to socialize, which fed into my withdrawal from society. Whenever we did visit with friends, I had trouble stringing two sentences together, my mouth felt locked. It was as though I were trapped in a glass jar, separate from others and alone. Afterward, it took me days to recover from the mental fatigue and physical exhaustion.

Noise and commotion were intolerable. Hyperaware of my breathing, I worried that I was breathing too fast or too slow, and that I might pass out and die. Sometimes, squiggly lines would form in my peripheral vision and reduce my eyesight to tunnel vision.

As much as I wanted to be everything for everybody, I couldn't. Fear and depression kept getting in my way, especially in the winter months when I suffered from seasonal affective disorder (SAD). According to a naturopath I consulted, in addition to SAD, he felt I was also hypersensitive to electrical smog.

A short while after I learned that anxiety had led my mother to quit driving, I had a severe anxiety attack while shopping.

There forward, I worried that I'd have to quit driving. Apparently, my grandmother had also suffered from anxiety. As anxiety wasn't yet recognized as a debilitating stressor, my mother and grandmother went undiagnosed for many years.

In 2011, Reid and I moved back to Victoria to be closer to family. Moving definitely helped my emotional health, however, after living in a quiet, sleepy community, the city was overwhelming.

Determined to help myself, in 2013, I enrolled in an online college program and obtained a degree in holistic nutrition. Although fear remained a vein that pulsed through my life, eating primarily organically-grown foods helped me physically and emotionally. Acutely aware that holistic nutrition was integral to regaining and sustaining optimal health, I started coaching others about the relationship between food and well-being. Still easily overwhelmed and often anxious, I was vigilant about getting enough sleep, not taking on too many clients, exercising regularly, and eating properly.

During my schooling, a childhood friend reached out to me. She had an autoimmune disease, and like me, continually researched alternative healing modalities. Having discovered and gained benefits from *pulsed electromagnetic field therapy* (PEMF therapy), she encouraged me to try this modality.

Open to the idea, I researched how PEMF therapy positively affected cells (the basic building blocks of all living things). From my schooling, I knew that the human body is composed of 75 trillion cells that provide structure for the body, take in nutrients from food, convert those nutrients into energy, and carry out specialized functions. The healthier your food choices, the healthier your body. Through my research, I learned that—

created by chemical reactions—the body's complex and carefully balanced superhighway of cells, tissue and fluid are affected by an array of electrical impulses. This biological whirlwind controls every cell, every nerve, every muscle, every thought. For example, the heart's natural pacemaker is electrically stimulated.

The company that manufactured the iMRS PEMF device I was researching claimed that their system produced an electromagnetic field that delivered frequencies that were healthy for the human body. This field penetrated deep inside the body to energize cells. Only stimulating healthy cells, not unhealthy cells, it had been scientifically proven that PEMF therapy accelerated healing and regeneration. By increasing metabolic functioning at a cellular level, the therapy expelled toxins that led to disease, and increased the body's oxygen supply and nutrition absorption.

Apparently the 3-way brainwave entrainment system with goggles and earphones could reduce depression and anxiety by altering the frequency of light patterns and colors, and by adjusting audible pulses and tones. I was intrigued but not convinced.

Six months later, following a severe bout of anxiety-riddled depression that strangled my ambitions and quality of life, I ordered the body mat and entrainment system.

The very first time I used the system, the electric-like current that continually buzzed through my body went quiet. I felt calm for four blissful hours. It was a degree of peaceful existence I'd never experienced. I was finally free of the overstimulation that kept me locked within my own body and separate from the world. Unable to wait for him to get home, I called Reid at work and told him how wonderful I felt. He was delighted for me. That night, I drifted off to sleep with renewed hope.

I started a routine of using the mat and entrainment system

twice daily. Every morning and evening, I reclined on the therapy mat and retreated into the soothing lights and sounds of the entrainment system for twenty minutes. Within a few weeks, my three-headed invisible monster was completely tamed.

I was happy, not depressed. Calm, not anxious. Actively engaged in life, not trapped in my home by agoraphobia. Instead of battling to barely exist in a world where I felt separate, alone and overstimulated, I could fully interact with my family, enjoy conversations with friends, and pursue my dreams.

When I looked back at my life, I couldn't find a time that I had felt the way I felt after a session on the mat. I must have exited the womb feeling anxious. Unable to cope with the ever-present fear, I'd become depressed, which led to agoraphobia. The pattern was likely the same for my mother and grandmother. There had to be some truth to scientific claims that emotional trauma is transmitted from generation to generation at a cellular level. Because it worked at a cellular level, PEMF therapy tamed my inner turmoil.

Having always sensed that there was a purpose or reason for the emotional stressors that I'd endured for the first thirty-seven years of my life, I opened Encompass Health & Wellness in 2016. Specializing in the two healing modalities that had helped me—holistic nutrition and pulsed electromagnetic field therapy—my heart sored as client after client reported positive results.

About three months into my new business, my husband came into my office and said that he was proud of me. It was the first time Reid had witnessed my abilities in sustained action. I smiled from ear to ear. I was accomplishing twenty times more than I could have handled in the past, and his recognition of my successes felt wonderful. If he was also worried that I might crash again, he kept it to himself.

Being one of the first practitioners to offer the iMRS and OMNIUM-1 system on Vancouver Island was both exciting and rewarding. I had found my calling and my passion. At the beginning of 2017, together with the founder, Wolfgang Jacksch, I hosted a wellness event at Camosun College in Victoria. Hearing this caring man's account of how pulsed electromagnetic field therapy helped him sustain his health following his battle with cancer inspired me further. I started travelling throughout North America sharing my story with wellness seekers and practitioners.

PEMF therapy balances the environment of one's body in whichever way is needed, emotionally and/or physically. I worked with clients with a myriad of conditions including arthritis, autoimmune disease, autism, back pain, depression, and numerous other afflictions. I also worked with clients who, like me, felt the joy of taking off the cloak of anxiety and feeling free. Clients whose pain level was ten out of ten and who had nearly given up hope discovered that PEMF was a sustainable solution that allowed them to start living with less pain, sometimes pain free. It warmed my heart that I was able to be a part of many people's paths to a better quality of life.

In 2017, Reid quit his full-time job and became actively involved in the business. Being able to work together was a goal we set when we left England. He's dedicated to us growing our business and to our family. He coaches our daughter's basketball team and ensures she's happy and healthy. As he works from home, when I travel, he is able to be there for Milly whenever she needs him.

I feel like I'd need a telescope to look back to where I was five years ago. Although there are times when I extend myself too far, whenever I start to feel overwhelmed, I tweak my schedule and take a day off. I get anxious when I'm about to take the stage but realize that most people are nervous about speaking in public. Thanks to my holistic diet and continued twice-daily use of the OMNIUM-1 PEMF mat and iMRS brainwave entrainment system, I am living a full life and realizing my dream to help others. My three-headed dragon is long slain. I am a "whole" me.

About Lindsay Laycock-Pirie

Lindsay Laycock-Pirie is a registered holistic nutritionist and a PEMF (Pulsed Electromagnetic Field) specialist. Lindsay, her husband, Reid, and their daughter, Milly, live in Victoria, British Columbia.

In addition to helping others and spending time with family and friends, Lindsay enjoys hiking, reading and baking.

Connect with Lindsay Laycock-Pirie
E-Mail: lindsaypirierhn@gmail.com
Facebook: www.facebook.com/lindsay.laycockpirie
Website: www.encompasshealthandwellness.org

Journey #12

SECRETS OF BEING ME

Margit Cleven

What am I going to do when I grow up?

What I wondered at thirteen years of age was a common refrain for me for decades. Now sixty-eight, I don't plan on ever growing up. It was a long journey, and for the most part, I like myself and my life.

In 1948, Mom and Dad were married in Lillooet, British Columbia. A short while later, they moved to the Bridge River area at the other end of Seton Lake. My dad was an electrician, and a long-time employee of BC Hydro and its predecessor, BC Electric. He was part of the crew that built what eventually became three dams that store water for four generating stations.

While I was a toddler, Dad's changing job sites resulted in my parents moving from place to place. They settled back in Bridge River when I was five. With only an elementary school, older kids were sent to a boarding school in Lillooet. After I completed grade four, Mom insisted we move to a larger town with a high school. The idea of sending her kids away didn't sit well with her.

We moved to Ruskin in 1963. Another very small community located on the outskirts of Mission and part of the Lower Mainland of Vancouver, British Columbia. Growing up in the sixties in a remote community of hydro brats came with benefits and hazards.

Ruskin didn't have any amenities, not even a gas station. We were bussed to school. If we wanted a chocolate bar, we walked two miles to the Ruskin corner store, ate our treat, and walked back home. No one worried about putting on weight. Our treats were guilt-free calories.

Long before cablevision, a small antenna commonly called rabbit ears sat on top of our bulky television set. Shows were only in black and white, and the reception was grainy. Broadcast hours were limited. If you turned on the television when nothing was being aired, an Indian-head test pattern would show on the screen accompanied by a high-pitched noise.

Saturday morning cartoons were the highlight of the week. When *Bonanza* or *The Ed Sullivan Show* aired, our entire family gathered around the television. When TV dinners began popping up in commercials, although they seemed like a great idea, they weren't a luxury my parents could afford.

Shortly after moving to Ruskin, I became friends with two sisters. Colleen was the same age as me, and her sister, Morven, was one year older. We had fun together. As the sisters had different interests, I'd sometimes hang out with one, not both. Careful not to hurt either's feelings, I'd then arrange an outing with the other.

Our circle of friends included lots of kids. Ken, David and Julie—my Mom's best friend's children who I thought of as a band of merry men—were always around and always fun to be with. Four older boys, Philip B., Philip N., Alan N., and Danny G. eventually joined our group.

Philip and Alan N. lived a few houses down on a farm. Philip N. wasn't modest, and I often spotted him shirt on, pants off. Cute, funny and flirtatious, and three or four years older than me, Philip N. was the first older boy to excite my hormones. I wasn't alone. Philip N. was every local girl's favorite crush.

Ruskin was a kid's utopia. The first summer there, while Dad was at work and Mom busy unpacking and organizing our new home, my brothers and I explored our huge yard and new neighborhood. We caught snakes and kept them in a wooden moving crate. Whenever my brothers wanted to scare the daylights out of me, they would stuff a snake down my shirt. Much to their delight, I'd scream and jump until the slithery creature fell out. Laughing, my brothers would take off running, me hot on their trail, hollering threats of their demise. It's probably a good thing that I never caught up with them until long after I cooled down.

There was a creek in our backyard. I loved the smell of the ferns growing along the bank and often made a bouquet with them. In the spring, my bouquets included wild pink roses. Together, they were beautiful and heavenly scented. The first summer we lived there, my brothers and I set up a table at the end of our driveway and tried to sell them. We weren't successful.

The following summer, we moved a few houses down. I was twelve, my brothers were eleven and nine. In Mom's eyes, we were ready for more freedom. Every sunny morning, we'd have breakfast, put on our swimsuits, walk a short way to where there was a pathway to the river, make our way down the hill and jump in the icy water. Friends also old enough to venture out on their own would be there too. Whenever my brothers and I got hungry, we went home, and Mom made us lunch.

Our house had one bathroom and a coal burning stove in the kitchen that served as the main heat source. Mom was always the first one to get up and would light the stove. Next, Dad got ready for work before enjoying the breakfast Mom made for him. When the three of us kids got up, the bathroom became a coveted room as we jockeyed for our turn to use the facilities. By the time we sat down at the table for a breakfast of oatmeal or cream of wheat, the kitchen was warm and cozy. A short while later, we'd head out the door to catch the school bus, the lunches Mom had made us wrapped in waxed paper and safely tucked inside a brown paper bag.

I thought my parents were perfect. Following along with what I believed was the way of the world, I wanted to be just like them. My thirteen-year-old goal was to have a boyfriend (when I was allowed to date), finish high school, get a job, get engaged, get married, have children and live happily ever after.

It was the era of "good girls" and "bad girls." Whenever anything sexual was discussed, which wasn't often, it was wrapped in shame, its bow a colorful story about some poor girl whose life shipwrecked when she got pregnant. There was no mistaking what choices I should make regarding boys and my body. What wasn't discussed, was what I should do when choices were taken from me.

For most of my young life, I was a follower and went along with just about anything that my friends wanted to do, whether I was comfortable with it or not. Though there were times when being a follower led to mistakes and heartache, following without questioning also led to my first official kiss.

One fall afternoon, Philip N. asked if I wanted to meet him under the BC Hydro carpenter shop that evening. Without thinking about it and flattered, I said, "Sure. What time?" Chubby and insecure, I hated my body and wasn't wild about me as a person. For me, being asked out by an older boy was proof that I was attractive, at least to him.

After dinner that evening, I told my mom I wanted to go out. Even though it was dark outside, she said I could go. Off I went to my pre-arranged meeting with Philip N. When we kissed, my world opened to exciting sensations and guilt.

It wasn't my first kiss, just the first I wanted. When I was nine years old, a babysitter in Bridge River had repeatedly insisted on having sex with me. Fearful of disobeying my elders, especially someone my parents liked, his taking advantage of my innocence went on for over a year. Not a hundred percent certain it wasn't my fault and afraid to disappointment my parents, I never told anyone what the sitter was doing.

Smoking was another secret I kept from my parents for as long as possible. The kids I hung out with in grade eight smoked. Unable to afford cigarettes, a girlfriend and I smoked porous reeds and sticks we found by the river's edge. Thanks to money earned from babysitting, by grade nine, I was hanging out with other students that smoked. Finally, I was part of the cool crowd. When Mom found a pack of smokes under my pillow, a long discussion ensued. After listening to me, she gave me permission to smoke at home, saying she'd didn't want me hanging out with the wrong crowd just so I could smoke.

Always wanting to protect me from situations that might lead me astray, in grade eleven, when a girlfriend asked me to join her on a week-long summer camping trip, Mom arranged for me to instead visit with my dad's relatives in Montreal.

I didn't share her fears about what might happen to me. From a young age, I felt protected by what could only have been an angel. When I was four or five, a man with a long cloak protected me as I rode on a horse and carved things out of bars of soap. When I was a teenager, I envisioned my ever-present protector as a fearless detective who would fend off anyone who might cause me harm. On the train ride to Montreal, my great protector was the real conductor.

Mom settled me into a seat on the train with well-wishes and a huge basket filled with sandwiches, fresh fruit and homemade cookies. That's when I realized that the trip from Vancouver to Montreal was going to be a long one. At least I was going to eat well.

In Manitoba, two young men got on the train. When a girl I'd met earlier introduced them to me, I locked eyes with the taller one. It was lust at first sight. The trip seemed to be picking up a bit!

After chatting with the three of them for hours, the girl told me that the two guys had just been released from a maximum security prison. I was surprised, but not overly concerned. If they tried to do me harm, my imaginary detective would intervene. When one of the guys told us that he'd bought a bottle of rye at the station we'd just stopped at and invited us to have a drink in the dome car, off we all went.

Since leaving Vancouver, I'd been unable to hold anything substantial on my stomach. It could have been motion sickness. More likely it was from wolfing down a half dozen cookies the first hour I was on the train. Whatever the reason for my empty stomach, the first few swigs of rye from the bottle had me giggling. The next few had me slurring. The next had me kissing the tall, good looking ex-convict. When I headed down the stairs to use the ladies' room, my legs refused to work, and I fell to the bottom.

When the conductor helped me to my feet and asked if I was okay, I thanked him and assured him I was *great*. I guess he didn't think I was doing as well as I thought I was. He helped me to the bathroom, waited for me, walked me back to my seat and told me not to move until next morning. I did as I was told. My friends joined me a while later, but there was no more drinking and no more kissing. *Shucks.*

I had a wonderful month experiencing life in Quebec. However, I was glad to get back home and settle into my final year of school. The quicker I was finished with my education, the sooner I could get on with my plan to get married, move to the suburbs, and have children.

Still struggling with my weight and excited about graduating, I went shopping for a fancy dress. Nothing fit. Mom sewed a beautiful gown for me to wear. She and Dad attended the ceremony, both of them visibly proud when I walked across the stage to receive my certificate.

My dad arranged for me to work at BC Hydro. I was scared to death about my new adventure but settled in well. During the summer, I met a young man, Henry, and we started dating. When BC Hydro transferred me to the Vancouver office, I moved in with my aunt to be closer to work. Henry lived four miles away. For me it was a win-win. I didn't have to travel as far for work, and I could see my boyfriend every night.

When Henry suggested we live together, I hesitated. My parents were churchgoers. It was the late sixties, and older adults viewed unmarried cohabitation as living in sin. Forever a pleaser, not wanting to disappoint my boyfriend, I suggested that the two of us talk to my mother about the idea.

Mom was mortified. After a heated discussion, she made me promise not to tell my dad. When we left my parents' place, Henry drove me back to my aunt's house. Living together wasn't an option. Having witnessed how upset Mom was, I didn't want her to worry or be disappointed in me.

Mom didn’t get the memo. She didn't understand that Henry

and I were asking for her blessing, not telling her a foregone conclusion. After we left her house, worried that I might run away, Mom drove around Vancouver searching for me. When she later told me about her search, I asked her why she hadn't simply called my aunt's place. She didn't have an answer.

A few months later, my brother Andy and I rented a basement suite. No longer under an adult's watchful eye, Henry often spent the night. Shortly after we moved in, my dad asked to stay over for a couple of days. He was attending an event in Vancouver, and he didn't want to daily make the commute from home, which was about an hour away.

For the few nights that Dad was there, when it was time for bed, after saying goodnight, Henry exited the suite via the backdoor, walked around the house to my bedroom window, and climbed through.

Months later, when Henry and I officially moved in together, we hid it from my entire family. Mom didn't always telephone before coming to visit. Sometimes she'd just drop by. Thankfully, by then, we lived on the third floor of an apartment with a controlled entrance and no elevator. Mom had to buzz my apartment to get in. By the time she climbed the two flights to our floor, Henry's belongings were hidden.

I didn't need a piece of paper to prove my commitment to Henry. Although she never knew we were cohabiting, Mom continually encouraged us to get married.

A year after Dad died, Henry and I decided to get legally hitched. Still struggling with my weight, my self-esteem was low, and I dreaded the idea of being the center of attention at a huge wedding. We were married at Mom's house with a few family members in attendance, followed by a small reception at the Elks Hall in Mission. During the ceremony, Mom was in seventh heaven. As I walked toward the minister in the beautiful gown Mom had made me for me, I was scared to death. While saying our vows, Henry and I both got the giggles. In an attempt to calm me, Mom gently poked me in the back and told me to shush. When the ceremony completed, Henry and I were more than ready to party with the eighty friends and relatives at the Elks Hall.

In the beginning, married life was great. We honeymooned in California a few months after our wedding and took other trips. We socialized with family and friends and looked forward to having kids. With the exception of our differing opinions on how clean and tidy the house needed to be, we were happy.

We were both delighted when I became pregnant. Our family and friends held baby showers, and Henry and I chatted about how we'd raise our children. Of utmost importance to me was protecting them from physical and emotional harm.

When our daughter, Carrie, was born we settled into baby mode. I watched her like a hawk. At the time, babies were occasionally being kidnapped from North American hospitals. Wanting her to have fresh air while I cleaned, I'd sometimes place Carrie in her pram by the opened front door with the screen door locked. Although she wasn't out of my sight, I didn't want to chance someone snatching her from our home.

Twenty-two months later, our son, Peter, joined our family. We seldom went out without our children, but when we did, Mom was our primary babysitter. When they were older, our kids went on playdates, but only when they were picked up and dropped off.

Like many married couples, Henry and I found more and more things to argue about. When he decided to sell our house, move our family into a townhouse and use the money we'd make to invest in his business, I was devastated. My utopian lifestyle was miles from how I'd imagined it would be. I still struggled with my weight and sense of self-worth. Whenever my husband hurt my feelings, I sunk a little further into what was likely undiagnosed depression. We separated in 1984, fourteen years after we met in 1970.

When Henry and I separated, I started working fulltime. Peter was in kindergarten and Carrie was in grade two. Having always walked my kids to and from school, I hired a sitter and insisted she do the same.

Thirty-two years old, my dream of having a husband and two children realized and then vaporized, I revamped my vision for the future. During the next decade, I searched for happiness of a different kind. Although men were suddenly pursuing me, I didn't want a permanent relationship. I enrolled in dance lessons at a local hālau (hula school) and started socializing. The kids stayed with their father every other weekend. On weekends when they were with me, Mom sometimes watched them when I also began dancing with a folk dance club. It was an exciting time filled with new adventures. Between working, caring my for children and exploring life, I functioned on little sleep. As much fun as I had, I wasn't happy.

As the years rolled on, I partnered with a few men who soon reinforced my conviction to stay single. Apparently, whatever I was searching for on a deeper level didn't come with a pair of trousers. However, still trying to fit into the norm, I remarried fifteen years after leaving my first husband.

Although we had a lot of fun in the beginning, somewhere in that marriage, I totally lost myself. Our differing goals and the ever-increasing emotional distance between my husband and me led to us parting ways.

I went back to work fulltime but retired early. As I needed to supplement my retirement income, I took a nail technician course and an income tax preparation course. I didn't enjoy working with people's fingernails, so I didn't become a nail technician. I did go to work in a tax office.

In 2011, a longtime friend talked me into attending her meditation group where I developed a few wonderful friendships. Two years later, I became a reiki master. I also started creating and marketing jewelry, bookmarks and energy/light-catchers made from crystals and gemstones.

Older and wiser, I'm no longer consumed with the idea of marriage as a means to an end. Although I continue to search for a deeper understanding of my place in the world, I've come to know that my happiness rests with me, not some ultimate goal or ideal life adopted in youth.

Rather than seek fulfillment through any individual, I find joy through interacting with others, spending time with family and friends, travelling, and through participating in a variety of activities. The secrets of being me no longer involves concealing what I'm up to from others or keeping quiet about what I think and believe. Most importantly, I embrace what is, not what could be.

"Gratitude is a powerful catalyst for happiness.
It's the spark that lights a fire of joy in your soul."
—Amy Collett

About Margit Cleven

Margit Cleven lives in Pitt Meadows, British Columbia. She has two children and three grandchildren. Semi-retired, Margit works part-time as a bookkeeper and tax consultant. She also markets her crystal and gemstone creations through trade fairs.

Time-permitting, Margit enjoys creating art stamp greeting cards, painting, and listening to country music. She is currently working on a series of short stories and an inspirational cookbook.

Margit's chapter in *Earth Angels #1*, "A Mother Grizzly Bear's Love," is a poignant (often humorous) tribute to her mom, Cecelia Cleven (known as Perry to her friends). As the title implies, her mother was a grizzly bear when it came to caring for her children, and where possible, protecting them from harm. When her mother died, Margit hoped that she had exited the world without awareness of some of the dangerous activities her kids had braved with great enthusiasm.

Margit is actively involved in her community. For a few years, she was on the executive committee of the Backstage Club of Vancouver and wrote and published their newsletters. She was the secretary-treasurer for the Ridge Meadows Opry for eight years. In support of the opry's fundraising endeavors, she co-created a cookbook featuring the *casts' and friends'* favorite recipes.

Always ready to offer a helping hand, Margit regularly provides bartending, DJ and karaoke services at gatherings hosted by her housing co-operative. Fun-loving, she embodies the saying, "If you don't grow up by the time your sixty, you don't have to."

Connect with Margit Cleven
E-Mail: margit.cleven@shaw.ca
Facebook: https://www.facebook.com/crystalengenz

Journey #13

VISITS FROM THE OTHER SIDE

Tara Diana Nagy

My name is Tara Diana and I'm a medium. (Ha-ha, it's as though I'm confessing to something.) *How do I know that you might ask?* Because I can communicate with spirits, people that are on the other side.

As far back as I can remember, I've *seen, heard, felt* and *known* things without an earthly reason for why I know what I know. You'd think having this ability would have helped me be the absolute best I could be, but it didn't. When young, being a medium never frightened me, it confused me as I struggled to make heads or tails of what was going on in my mind.

People often ask if being a spiritual medium runs in my family. If you met my sister, Paula, you would definitely know that it does. If you spent time with my mother, you'd soon learn that her intuition is topnotch. For various reasons, neither of these lovely ladies uses her abilities, but both are highly intuitive.

I've never slept well. Since I was four years old, I've had what others might call "imaginary friends." As there was too much going on in my room, when I was little, I would wait until my parents fell asleep and then sneak into their bedroom and curl up on the small blue rug at the side of their bed. When I started school, I went to bed with the light off and the door open. Once everyone else was asleep, I quietly shut my door and played with the visiting spirits until early morning.

Although I didn't recognize the cause of my challenges at the time, not getting enough sleep and having nighttime visitors wreaked havoc on my psyche. I was always anxious and constantly worried. I fretted over my ability to do homework. Sensing that I was different, although I had friends, I worried whether other kids thought I was weird or odd.

I was an adult when I learned it was possible to set boundaries with spirits that choose inappropriate times or places to make their presence known. I also came to know that mediumship is a gift meant to be shared with others through readings, and that though I'm somewhat unique, there are numerous others who possess similar abilities.

I'm from a small family of four. Three years younger than me, my sister, Paula, has been a huge part of my life. She's always helped me to stay grounded, which was especially helpful when my kids were young.

Our parents are both twins, and our father is an identical twin. When Paula and I were young, there were frequent family gatherings with our great-grandmother, grandparents and many aunts, uncles and cousins. Our family was especially close to Nana and Papa on our father's side.

Our father and his brother have always been extremely close. They worked at the same place and bought vacation homes at the same location. Throughout their lives, they've shared a great desire to be with their parents, Robert (Bud) and Mildred. When our father and his brother moved into their own places, they were so close to their parents that they went to their parents' house every day *before* and *after* work to play cards with them.

I have many fond memories of Nana and Papa. Of Ukrainian descent, Nana was born in Manitoba. She worked in a factory and was the most industrious person I've ever known. When her sons lived at home, she mended their work overalls by hand and washed their clothes in a big tub in the basement of their home. When Paula and I were little, Nana sewed our Barbie Doll clothes by hand.

Nana made the best cabbage rolls and pedaheh (perogies) and meatballs. She also made the best macaroni and egg casserole. Her pies were like no other. The first thing I noticed whenever I walked into their home was the delicious smell of whatever she'd prepared for our meal. When someone in my family commented about how good it smelled, Papa would claim that he'd spent hours making it, and Nana would grumble good-naturedly as she swatted him with a dishtowel. Despite taking undue credit for Nana's cooking, Papa was incredibly kind, except when someone was beating him at cards or Yahtzee—then, it was all gloves off!

Christmas Eve was always celebrated at Nana and Papa's home with our family and Dad's brother's family. Whatever the occasion, whenever our families gathered together at their home, it was a warm and happy time. Like my cousins did with their spouses and children, when I married and had Alanna and Ryan, my husband and I continued to visit Nana and Papa on Christmas Eve. Busy raising my own family, as time passed, I was unable to visit with them as often as I'd have liked. Paula, however, made it her mission to visit and help them as often as she could.

Paula resonated with the elderly in our family. When Nana started to suffer from dementia, Paula helped our dad and his twin brother look after Nana and Papa. She even took a care aid course so that she knew how to properly care for them and our great-aunt on our mother's side. When Nana died, Paula dedicated herself to helping Papa.

Extremely lonely without his wife, poor Papa tended his garden, watched wrestling with Paula, and played with the two geriatric cats my sister adopted for him. While everyone did their best to be there for Papa, it was Paula who visited and cared for him the most.

When Papa was hospitalized with stomach issues, Mom told me he was seeing "things" and Paula told me he was seeing "spirits." I believe he even saw cats. Having heard that the spirits of loved ones often visit the dying, I concluded that Papa was nearing the end of his earthly journey. Although we didn't talk about it, I suspected everyone in the family was expecting the same outcome.

One evening, my husband, Mike, and I took our kids to a Red Robin restaurant for dinner. Mike and Alanna were seated opposite Ryan and me when I suddenly felt uncomfortable and cold. Wondering if he was cold too, I glanced up from the menu and looked at my husband. When I did, I saw two people standing beside him. My breath caught in my throat as I took a moment to center myself and discern whether I was seeing spirits.

I recognized the elderly man as my Papa's brother Norman who at the ripe old age of one hundred had recently passed away. The slightly older than middle-aged woman standing next to him was dressed in clothes reminiscent of the late fifties. I was aware that Mike was looking my way as I stared at the spirits staring at me, when the woman smiled and said, "Your grandfather is going to cross over in twenty minutes." Then Norman said, "Call your sister and tell her not to leave the hospital. She should be there with him when he goes. He would like that." And with that, they were gone.

Although I'd had all sorts of weird interactions with those on the other side, family spirits generally let me be. Stunned, it took a moment for me to fully comprehend what I'd heard and grab my cell phone. When Mike asked who I was calling, I said, "Paula! Papa is going to die in twenty minutes, and I need to tell her so she can be with him!" Thank goodness our kids were little and not paying attention or they may have thought their mother was a bit loopy.

When Paula answered the phone, I asked her where she was.

"I'm just about to leave the hospital. My parking meter is about to run out."

"You can't leave. Papa is going to go in twenty minutes," I said, sounding much more collected than I felt.

"Do I have enough time to feed the meter?" she asked, not a hint of doubt in her voice as to whether I was right about our Papa.

After graciously waiting for Paula to feed the parking meter, with her whispering loving words in his ear, our kind and gentle Papa passed away twenty minutes after I called my sister. Mike and the kids dropped me off at the hospital twelve minutes after he passed. Mom, Dad and his brother and his family arrived about thirty minutes later.

Papa's passing unfolded just as the spirits of his brother Norman and the woman said they should, with his granddaughter at his side. Undoubtedly, their message made my grandfather's transition easier for him and for Paula. After much thought, I came to believe that the woman spirit was my grandfather's mother, my great-grandmother. I will be eternally grateful for that moment in Red Robin and the visit from our ancestors on the other side.

About Tara Diana Nagy

Tara Diana Nagy is a sought-after medium and psychic. She and her family live in Burnaby, British Columbia. Actively involved in her children's lives, she often posts about their accomplishments and activities on Facebook. Having long learned how set boundaries with spirits, Tara Diana sometimes jokes that her sleepless nights are now a result of having teenage children, not visits from spirits.

Tara Diana is passionate about helping people and animals, especially children with challenges and rescue dogs in need of homes. Her favorite pastimes include being in nature and spending time with family and friends.

On a mission to empower others through mediumship and natural products, she is the owner of Spirit Essence by Tara Diana. She is also the co-owner of T & T Spiritual Wellness Connections, which regularly hosts metaphysical fairs where attendees can shop for products to enhance their well-being and interact with intuitive readers, psychics, mediums, and healers.

Connect with Tara Diana Nagy
E-Mail: taraangelreadings@live.com
Website: http://www.tandtvancouver.com
Facebook: www.facebook.com/spiritessencebytaradiana/

HEARTMIND STORE
Boutique-Style Online Bookstore

Connecting Readers & Authors in a Deep and Meaningful Way.

Website: www.heartmindstore.com
E-Mail: info@heartmindstore.com

“If stories come to you, care for them.
And learn to give them away where they are needed.
Sometimes a person needs a story more than food
to stay alive.” —Barry López

Made in the USA
Monee, IL
01 July 2021

72752644R00118